A Method of Programming

A Method of Programming

Edsger W. Dijkstra
University of Texas at Austin

W. H. J. Feijen
Technical University of Eindhoven

Translated by Joke Sterringa

ADDISON-WESLEY
PUBLISHING
COMPANY

Wokingham, England · Reading, Massachusetts · Menlo Park, California
New York · Don Mills, Ontario · Amsterdam · Bonn
Sydney · Singapore · Tokyo · Madrid · San Juan

The programs presented in this book have been included for their instructional
value. They have been tested with care but are not guaranteed for any particular
purpose. The publisher does not offer any warranties or presentations, nor does it
accept any liabilities with respect to the programs.

Cover designed by Crayon Design of Henley-on-Thames
and printed by The Riverside Printing Co. (Reading) Ltd.
Typeset by Columns of Reading
Printed in Great Britain by T.J. Press (Padstow), Cornwall

The original Dutch edition of this book was published in The Netherlands:
Een methode van programmeren. Edsger W. Dijkstra and W.H.J. Feijen.
The Hague: Academic Service, 1984.

First English edition printed 1988.

British Library Cataloguing in Publication Data
Dijkstra, Edsger W.
    A method of programming.
    1. Computer systems. Programming.
    Applications of mathematical logic
    I. Title   II. Feijen, W.H.J.   III. Een
    methode van programmeren. *English*
    005.13'1

ISBN 0–201–17536–3

81 off 3/22/89

Library of Congress Cataloguing in Publication Data
Dijkstra, Edsger Wybe.
    [Methode van programmeren. English]
    A method of programming / Edsger W. Dijkstra. W.H.J. Feijen. –
1st English ed.
        p.   cm.
    Translation of: Een methode van programmeren.
    ISBN 0–201–17536–3
    1. Electronic digital computers—Programming   I. Feijen, W.H.J.
    II. Title.
QA76.6.D5513 1988
005. 1—dc19   88–1580 CIP

Preface

This text was originally written under relatively high pressure, when a computer science curriculum was thrust upon us rather suddenly. The reason for writing it was the same as the reason why we later agreed to have a second version of it published as a book: the text fulfils what we have come to regard as a serious need.

Programming started out as a craft which was practised intuitively. By 1968 it began to be generally acknowledged that the methods of program development followed so far were inadequate to face what then appeared as the so-called 'software crisis'. After the methods then employed had been identified as fundamentally inadequate, a style of design was developed in which the program and its correctness argument were designed hand in hand. This was a dramatic step forward.

Although it appears in monographs and textbooks, this achievement has not yet reached the introductory programming curriculum. What, for lack of a better term, we shall call 'the computer science boom' induced us to end this situation, for two reasons. Firstly, the growing number of students makes it increasingly unjustifiable to organize the introductory curriculum according to an obsolete model. Secondly, with the growing popularity of computers, the traditionally intuitive introduction contributes less and less to the further education of the student.

It is for these reasons that, in this text, programming is presented as what it has since become – a formal branch of mathematics, in which mathematical logic has become an indispensable tool.

The book consists of two parts, originally corresponding to the lectures and their instruction, respectively. The lectures unfold the subject matter that is specific to programming, while the instruction describes the logical apparatus used for this and contains the exercises. How the reader may best divide his or her attention between the two parts is optional, since the optimum balance will depend on the reader's background.

We owe thanks to all our colleagues in the Department of Computer Science at the Technical University of Eindhoven who have taught the subject described here with so much enthusiasm and success over the last few years. In particular, we would like to mention A. J. M. van Gasteren, A. Kaldewaij, M. Rem, J. L. A. van de Snepscheut and J. T. Udding. Their experience and stimulation have been a great support.

Eindhoven   Edsger W. Dijkstra
                                                              W. H. J. Feijen

Contents

PART 1

PART 0

A method of programming

'Informatics' is the name used since 1968 in non-Anglo-Saxon countries for the subject called 'computer science' in the USA and Great Britain. For the Anglo-Saxon term 'computer' Dutch uses 'automatic calculating machine' or the shorter 'calculating automaton'; both terms are adequate, provided that – as we shall see later – we do not assign too narrow a meaning to the concept of 'calculating'.

We use the term 'automaton' for a mechanism which, if so designed, can do something for us autonomously, that is, without any further interference on our part. A familiar automaton (at least in some countries) is, for example, the cistern of a toilet. After the starting signal – pulling the chain or pushing the button – the rest takes care of itself: the toilet is flushed clean, the cistern fills up and, at the right moment, the feed tap is closed so that the cistern does not overflow.

On this basis one may think that a cigarette machine would not deserve the name of automaton, which it has in Dutch, since the customer must interact in all kinds of ways: for example, he or she must insert coins and pull out a drawer. These actions, however, may be regarded as an elaborate starting signal: the machine is an automaton for the tobacconist, who is not disturbed at all during the transaction.

Other classic examples of automata are the clock and the music box, which if wound up plays 'O, du lieber Augustin'. (It was often the same craftsman who manufactured both music boxes and clocks, whether or not the clocks were provided with a cuckoo.)

The above mechanisms are a bit dull because, in some sense, they do the same each time: the cistern takes care of one flushing after another, the clock repeats its pattern every 12 hours, and the music box lets us have 'O, du lieber Augustin' *ad nauseam*. (Since Watt's steam engine also belongs to this group of dull mechanisms, we should not speak disrespectfully of this dullness.)

These mechanisms were succeeded by a more flexible type, for example, the type of music box with a changeable cylinder: this meant that 'O, du lieber Augustin' or 'Here we go round the mulberry bush'

3

could be performed with largely the same machine. Many automata are of this type: the pianola, the film projector, and the street organ. Again it does not become us to speak of them disrespectfully: Jacquard's loom and the modern automatic controlled milling machine come into this category, as do playback equipment for gramophone records, video discs, and tapes.

These mechanisms have been introduced to illustrate the concept of an automaton. They do not share the other aspect of the 'calculating automaton', namely that it 'calculates', so that now (with due respect) we take our leave from them.

What do we mean by 'calculate'? Let us take a very simple example: the addition of two natural numbers in the decimal system. Very simple? Maybe – though, after having learned the numbers 0 to 9, it still takes years before children get the hang of it (and some never do). Let us see what it takes.

To begin with we learn the tables of addition as shown in Figure 1.

	0	1	2	3	4	5	6	7	8	9
0	0	1	2	3	4	5	6	7	8	9
1	1	2	3	4	5	6	7	8	9	10
2	2	3	4	5	6	7	8	9	10	11
3	3	4	5	6	7	8	9	10	11	12
4	4	5	6	7	8	9	10	11	12	13
5	5	6	7	8	9	10	11	12	13	14
6	6	7	8	9	10	11	12	13	14	15
7	7	8	9	10	11	12	13	14	15	16
8	8	9	10	11	12	13	14	15	16	17
9	9	10	11	12	13	14	15	16	17	18

Figure 1

The upper row and the left-hand column are not very difficult, and gradually the child becomes familiar with the upper left corner of the table: the so-called 'calculating under ten'. After some time the bottom right corner also becomes familiar: the child now knows by heart the addition of two numbers under ten. This is very good: the child now knows the answer to 100 different additions.

However, it is also clear that we cannot go on like this. There are 10 000 different additions of two numbers less then 100, 1 000 000 different additions of two numbers less than 1000, and it would obviously be madness to try to learn such large tables by heart. Fortunately, we do not have to, for – as any schoolchild will have noticed – the table is not without regularity. The next stage in our addition education, therefore, consists of learning to exploit this regularity.

To begin with, we do not regard larger numbers as an entity, but as a series of digits, which are dealt with one by one: we learn to construct the sequence of digits that represents the sum from the sequences of digits which represent the numbers to be added.

What are the ingredients of this construction process? First the digits of the numbers to be added are added two by two. This is represented by writing the numbers one under the other. And for this we learn that 2037 + 642 should look like

    2037
    642

and *not* like

    2037
    642

This addition is easy, because for each pair we can do our calculations 'under ten':

    2037
    642
    ———— +
    2679

and so far it does not matter if we work from left to right or from right to left.

To be able to execute additions like

    2037
    645
    ———— +
    2682

as well, the rules are extended with 'carry 1', and to cap it all the pupil is made familiar with the cascade phenomenon which occurs when 'carry 1' must be applied in a position where the sum of the digits is 9, as in:

    2057
    645
    ———— +
    2702

This extensive examination of the decimal addition of two natural numbers is useful not because it is presupposed that the reader cannot add, but to provide an awareness of the many rules that are applied, albeit virtually unconsciously.

If formulated with sufficient precision, such a combination of rules makes up what we call an **algorithm**. (Above we have informally given an algorithm for the decimal addition of natural numbers.) An algorithm is a prescription which, provided it is faithfully executed, yields the desired result in a finite number of steps.

With reference to the addition algorithm given, we can at once make the following remark.

Remark. It is not necessarily true that an algorithm leaves nothing to the imagination of the one who carries it out: irrelevant choices may be left open. In order to add 2057 and 645, the numbers are written one under the other, but evidently,

$$\begin{array}{r} 2057 \\ 645 \\ \hline 2702 \end{array} + \qquad \text{and} \qquad \begin{array}{r} 645 \\ 2057 \\ \hline 2702 \end{array} +$$

do equally well. In the corresponding multiplication algorithm this phenomenon is more marked. Compare:

$$\begin{array}{r} 71 \\ 28 \\ \hline 568 \\ 142 \\ \hline 1988 \end{array} * \qquad \text{and} \qquad \begin{array}{r} 28 \\ 71 \\ \hline 28 \\ 196 \\ \hline 1988 \end{array} *$$

∎

Remark. The addition algorithm can be applied in a great many different cases. The fact that, as in this example, the algorithm is applicable in an unlimited number of cases, and that, independent of the numbers to be added, there is no upper bound for the number of steps an execution of the algorithm will take, does not alter the fact that any individual execution takes only a finite number of steps. ∎

Another algorithm is illustrated by the composition of differentiation rules which, for example, enables us to compute

$$\frac{d}{dx} (e^{\sin x})$$

as:

$$(\cos x) \cdot e^{\sin x}$$

The differentiation algorithm allows some freedom concerning the order in which the various rules are applied and is, in principle, also applicable in an unlimited number of cases. This example is included because, while it is customary to speak of 'the computation of a derivative', the computing is here already stripped of any specific numerical associations.

Other examples of algorithms are planimetric constructions (for the bisector of an angle, the apex of a triangle, etc.), knitting patterns, user instructions, assembly instructions, recipes, and the rules we follow to see if someone is listed in the telephone directory.

Remark. For the telephone directory of Amsterdam the rules are simpler, and searching generally does not take quite as many steps as it does for the 1982 telephone directory for Eindhoven and Region, in which the names of subscribers are listed according to their villages. The design of the latter directory may be considered to be faulty.   ■

The automatic calculating machine is so called because it can 'calculate' automatically in the sense of carrying out an algorithm automatically. The computer derives its great flexibility from the fact that the selection of the algorithm to be carried out by the mechanism is up to us, and that in selecting this algorithm we have virtually unlimited freedom. (Compared with the mechanisms mentioned before, the computer represents a quantum leap.)

We can express the fact that the computer can be fed with an algorithm of our choice by saying that the computer is 'programmable'. An algorithm that could be executed by a mechanism is called a 'program', and to design programs is called 'to program'. Programming is the main subject of these lectures.

Programming merits a lecture course for a. number of reasons. First of all, there is always a program needed to bridge the gap between the general-purpose computer and the specific application, and therefore the activity of programming takes a central place. Second, we know from experience that someone who has not learned to think and reason sufficiently pragmatically and soundly about the design during the programming, will irrevocably make a mess of things. To make the student completely familiar with the most effective known way of reasoning about algorithms is therefore an important objective of this course.

One warning is called for: a program is a formal text in which each letter, each digit, each punctuation mark and each operator plays its part. Programs must therefore be written with uncommon precision. Since most people grow up with the idea that they can get away with a few mistakes of spelling or grammar here and there in their writings, and behave accordingly, they are often taken aback by this requirement for precision on their first introduction to programming; so much so that they think programming is a matter of accuracy only. Once this accuracy has become second nature, they realize that the difficulty lies somewhere else completely: in the duty to prevent the subject from becoming unmanageably complicated. (Some inexperienced people regard the necessity for this accuracy as a fault in the computer, but they do not realize that the computer derives its usefulness from the very faithfulness with which it executes the algorithm assigned to it, and *no other*.)

Finally, the student should realize that what can be dealt with in the narrow scope of this introductory course cannot be representative of programming in all its possible aspects. In order to save time, and not to make things unnecessarily difficult, we shall develop our programs for a very simple machine from which elaborate trimmings (which all too often prove to be snags) are missing. The particular difficulties of the development of really large programs are outside the scope of this introductory course.

Mechanisms and their states

Let us consider a mechanism which, once started, performs something for a while, and then stops. As examples, we can think of a gramophone or a toilet cistern. The gramophone is started by putting a disc on the turntable and lowering the stylus into the groove; it stops when, at the end of the groove, the stylus comes too close to the axis of the turntable. The cistern is started by pulling the chain; when the cistern has filled up again, the feed tap is closed, and the process is stopped.

A mechanism, if started, not only does something for a while and then stops, but also, since it is a mechanism, it does it automatically, that is, without further interaction on our part. Because of this, such a mechanism is in a *different* state at any moment between start and stop: shortly after starting, it is in a state such that it will go on for quite a while, and shortly before the end it is in a state such that it nearly stops.

Someone who knows the mechanism involved and knows where to look can always see how much progress the working mechanism has made. In the case of the gramophone the state of progress is reflected by the position of the arm: one look at its position is sufficient to determine how far the playing of the record has progressed.

Remark. At different moments between start and stop, the mechanism must be in different states. When, because of a scratch in the record, the needle clicks back to the last groove and the gramophone thus returns to a state it has previously been in, this condition is not fulfilled. There is something wrong: the needle is stuck and because it cannot progress it will not finish and stop automatically. ∎

In the case of the cistern, too, the state determines how far the autonomous process has progressed. The water level in the cistern, however, is only partially analogous to the position of the gramophone arm: during the whole cycle the cistern is half-full twice, once during emptying and once while filling up. The distinction between the two states is determined by the fact that the bell does or does not close off the drain pipe. We may conclude that the state of the cistern is approximately determined by two variables: the continuous variable of the 'water level' and the discrete variable 'drain', for which only the two values 'open' and 'closed' are available.

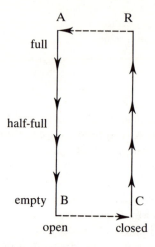

Figure 2

In Figure 2 the water level is represented vertically and the two states of the drain, open and closed, horizontally. Point R is the state of rest: cistern full and drain closed. The start, pulling the chain, opens the drain, which remains open as long as water flows through it with sufficient rapidity. When the cistern is empty, the bell drops again and the drain is closed, after which the cistern fills up. (The water supply is opened when the cistern is not full. The capacity of the supply, however, is smaller than that of the drain, so that the supply does not prevent the cistern from emptying. Verify that, when the capacity of the drain is twice that of the supply, flushing the toilet, i.e. traversing the path from A to B, takes as long as filling the cistern afterwards, i.e. traversing the path from C to R. From the fact that flushing generally takes much less time than the filling of the cistern afterwards, we may conclude that the ratio of the two capacities is usually considerably larger than 2.)

Any possible state of the cistern corresponds to a point in our two-dimensional figure, which has therefore been given the name of **state space**. (In this special case we may speak of a 'state plane', because the state space is two-dimensional. However, we shall use the more general term 'space', as in many cases our state space will have more than two dimensions.) The event which takes place in the period between start and stop is reflected in the form of a path in the state space which must be traversed. (Note that this path does not reflect the speed with which it is traversed.)

The position of a point in the state space is here denoted by two coordinates: the water level and the fact that the drain is open or closed. Here, the water level is a continuous variable and the state of the drain has been treated as a discrete variable, which has only the values open and closed. (This means that we regard opening and closing the drain as indivisible, instantaneous events: the drain is open or closed, but not half-open. This kind of 'point event' is a useful idealization, not unlike 'point mass' in classical mechanics.) With a view to the structure of computers, discussion will be confined to state spaces in which all coordinates are discrete. If, for example, the state space is spanned by two integer coordinates, i.e. limited to integer values, we can represent the state space by the grid points in the plane shown in Figure 3, and the path by 'jumps' from one grid point to another.

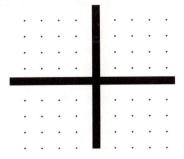

Figure 3

Remark. There are machines in which values are represented by continuously variable physical quantities, such as voltage, current intensity, or the rotation angle of an axis. These are the so-called **analogue** machines. They are completely outside the scope of this book. Analogue machines have always had the drawback that it is technically impossible in this way to represent values with very high precision. They have largely lost their earlier advantage of speed, as digital computers have become faster, so that what used to be done by analogue equipment is now carried out more and more by digital equipment – for example, the digital recording of music. ∎

Computation as a change of state

A computer reacts to signals it receives from the external world by giving signals in response to the signals received. Taking in information from the external world is called the **input**, and yielding information is called **output**. As part of the automation of 008 – the number for 'Information' of the Dutch telephone company – we can imagine a machine which takes as input the name and address of a subscriber, and returns the corresponding phone number as output to the external world.

The way in which input and output take place often differs from one computer to another. In automating telephone information, the input of name and address will probably be made by a telephone operator who 'types' this in via a keyboard (like that of a typewriter), while the output takes place by means of a screen, so that the operator can give the desired answer without having to leaf through large telephone directories. It is also conceivable that the computer could produce the answer in an audible form. The Girobank gives us an example where input and output take place through quite different channels: input takes place by means of punched cards (or other machine-readable forms), and output takes place by means of addressed and printed 'statements of account'.

Because of the large variety of input and output media we shall largely abstract from input and output in this course, and focus our attention on what goes on from the moment the input is completed and the computations can commence, to the moment the computations are completed, and the answer is ready for output.

Remark. For sake of simplicity we pass over the fact that the computation process can start in part before the input is completed, and that sometimes output of part of the answer is possible before the process of computation is completed. ∎

The reasons for confining ourselves to the period from the end of the input to the beginning of the output are many. Firstly, different computers resemble each other in what goes on internally far more than in the ways in which they communicate with the external world; what goes on internally is therefore a subject of a far more universal nature. Secondly, it is during this period that the real process of computation, on which we should focus our attention, takes place. (A third reason, which can be mentioned now but not yet explained, is that it is a simplification which enables us to treat partial computations on the same level as the total computation.)

In what follows we shall consider computational processes which start from an **initial state** of the mechanism and lead to a **final state** of the mechanism. If it concerns the whole computation, we shall tacitly assume from now on that the initial state is directly determined by the input and that the final state is directly determined by what must be the output.

A little more precisely: the initial and final states are described by the same set of coordinates for each computation, the input determines the value of one or more coordinates for the initial state, and in the final state the value of one or more coordinates represents the desired answer.

Remark. The input does not have to specify the values of all the coordinates. ∎

In deciding to regard computations as changes of state, we can give the **functional specification** of a program by stating the relation between the initial and the final state. A fixed plan for this functional specification will be used, and its description illustrated by a series of small examples.

Such a functional specification consists of four ingredients:

(i)   the **declaration** of **local variables**;

(ii) the precondition, traditionally put in braces;

(iii) the name of the program, traditionally separated from what went before by a semicolon;

(iv) the postcondition, also traditionally put in braces.

All this is preceded by the opening bracket |[(pronounced 'begin') and followed by the corresponding closing bracket]| (pronounced 'end').

A simple example of a functional specification is the following (in which, for the sake of discussion, the lines are numbered):

(i) |[x : int

(ii)   {x = X}

(iii)   ; skip

(iv) $\{x = X\}$

           $]|$

Remark. If the opening and closing brackets are not on the same line, they are vertically aligned for the sake of clarity. The functional specification given above is so small that there would have been no objection at all to the layout:

$|[$ x: int $\{x = X\}$; skip $\{x = X\}$ $]|$ ■

We should read this functional specification as follows. Line (i) tells us that it concerns a state space with only one coordinate, which is denoted by the name x, and whose value range is limited to integers. This is the purpose of the **type indication** : int, which concludes the declaration. (int is short for the Latin word *integer*.) The rest tells us that the original validity of precondition (ii) is sufficient for the execution of the program skip in line (iii), to ensure that afterwards postcondition (iv) will hold.

When, as is the case here, the conditions contain a quantity like X, which actually comes out of the blue, it means that the functional specification holds for any *possible* value of X. (Since x is integer and x = X, we do not have to worry about $X = 3\frac{1}{2}$.) In other words, the above functional specification of skip tells us that skip must leave the value of x, whatever it may be, unchanged.

Another simple example of a functional specification of a program, which we shall also conveniently call skip, is:

(i) $|[$ x, y, z: int

(ii) $\{x = X \quad \wedge \quad y = Y \quad \wedge \quad z = Z\}$

(iii)   ; skip

(iv) $\{x = X \quad \wedge \quad y = Y \quad \wedge \quad z = Z\}$

           $]|$

This specifies that in a three-dimensional state space with coordinates x, y and z execution of skip should leave the values of each of the coordinates, whatever they may be, unchanged.

Remark. The order in which, separated by commas, the local names x, y and z are listed in the declaration is irrelevant. Equivalent forms for line (i) are therefore:

$|[$ x, z, y: int
$|[$ z, y, x: int etc.

We have introduced the three local variables here together in one declaration. We could also have introduced each with its own declaration; in that case, however, such independent declarations must be separated by semicolons. For example:

|[x: int; y: int; z: int

Mixed forms are also permitted, as in:

|[x, y: int; z: int

EXERCISE

Check that, with the above-mentioned liberties, line (i) can be written in 24 different, but equivalent, ways.

If in a complicated program variables obviously belong together in groups, the clarity of the text may be enhanced by a corresponding declaration in groups. ∎

The declaration(s) is (are) always preceded by the opening bracket |[. The corresponding closing bracket]| indicates the point of the text up to which the meaning, which is assigned to the names introduced by the declaration, is applicable. In this way the pair of brackets |[and]| defines the scope of the names in the text.

Two specifications are given above, one for skip in a one-dimensional state space, and one for skip in a three-dimensional space. In this way we could define skip every time we introduce state spaces. Because this would become far too tedious, we consider skip as defined in *any* state space: from now on skip is the universal name of the action which does not effect any changes of state, irrespective of the state space used to define the state.

Remark. On the face of it skip does not seem to be terribly useful. Later we shall see that skip is just as useful as the digit 0 in the positional number system. ∎

Further examples of functional specifications are:

```
|[ x, y: int
    {x = x   ∧   y = Y}
; swap0
    {x = Y   ∧   y = X}
]|
```

and

```
|[ x, y: int
   {x = Y  ∧  y = X}
 ; swap1
   {x = X  ∧  y = Y}
]|
```

Show that the functional specifications of swap0 and swap1 are equivalent.

Programs swap0 and swap1 have the property that, on knowing the final state, the initial state can be deduced. If, for example, after execution of swap1 the state is given by x = 2 ∧ y = 3, we can conclude that in the initial state x = 3 ∧ y = 2. We can express this by saying that the execution of swap1 does not destroy any information, in contrast to the following programs, copy and euclid, for example.

```
|[ x, y: int
   {x = X}
 ; copy
   {x = X  ∧  y = X}
]|
```

If the outcome of copy is x = 5 ∧ y = 5 we may conclude that originally x = 5. With regard to the original value of y, which is *not* mentioned in the precondition, we cannot draw any conclusions; the value of y may therefore have been anything at the beginning.

```
|[ x, y: int
   {x = X  ∧  y = Y  ∧  x > 0  ∧  y > 0}
 ; euclid
   {x = y  ∧  x = gcd(X, Y) }
]|
```

In euclid, gcd stands for 'greatest common divisor of'. If the outcome of euclid is x = 5 ∧ y = 5, the initial state cannot have been anything whatsoever. For example, x = 40 ∧ y = 70 is out of the question, but there are many possibilities. We could have specified the same program euclid as follows:

```
|[ x, y: int
   {X = gcd(x, y)  ∧  x > 0  ∧  y > 0}
```

```
; euclid
   {x = X  ∧  y = X}
]|
```

Examination of the final state does determine the value of X, for example 5, but for a given value of X the precondition, regarded as an equation in the two unknowns x and y, has many solutions. So euclid also destroys information.

Remark. It is important to realize that an incorrect functional specification can make impossible demands, as in the following incorrect specification for root:

```
|[ x: int
   {x = X}
; root
   {x = √X}
]|
```

If originally x = 43, then for X = 43 the precondition is neatly fulfilled, but with this value of X the postcondition cannot be satisfied with integer x. (And the same holds when initially x is negative.) In short, the precondition above is too weak and must be strengthened with the additional condition that x is a square. If, as in this and most cases, the final state is uniquely determined by the initial state, the naming of the values in the final state is, as a rule, the easiest way to overcome this:

```
|[ x: int
   {x = X²  ∧  X ≥ 0}
; root
   {x = X}
]|
```

■

Programs and their construction

In the preceding section we saw that it is the objective of a computation to effect a change of state as laid down in a functional specification. Because, as a rule, such a functional specification contains a number of unspecified parameters – denoted in our examples by X, Y or Z – a functional specification usually describes a large class of changes of state. The program must indicate how these changes of state are to be effected.

For a limited class of changes of state this can be effected in a single step: the initial state is then directly rendered into the final state. Such computations take very little time; they correspond to the building blocks with which we can build complicated programs, which can give rise to longer computations. During such a longer computation the total change of state is effected by the succession of a (possibly large) number of 'small' changes, that is, changes that can be effected directly in one step. The corresponding blocks from which the program is constructed are called **assignment statements**, and the following section discusses how assignment statements are written in a program, and which changes of state correspond to each assignment statement.

Remark. Two-fold use is made of our formalism for functional specification. For euclid, the functional specification should be seen as the formulation of a programming exercise. For skip the functional specification was used for the definition of a building block available to the programmer. This latter use will be followed in the introduction of the assignment statement.

The assignment statement

Consider the functional specifications of the following programs which, for lack of imagination, we shall call S0, S1 and S2:

$$|[\; x, y: \text{int } \{X = 0 \quad \wedge \quad Y = y\}; \text{ S0 } \{X = x \quad \wedge \quad Y = y\} \;]|$$
$$|[\; x, y: \text{int } \{X = 88 \quad \wedge \quad Y = y\}: \text{ S1 } \{X = x \quad \wedge \quad Y = y\} \;]|$$
$$|[\; x, y: \text{int } \{X = x + 3 \quad \wedge \quad Y = y\}; \text{ S2 } \{X = x \quad \wedge \quad Y = y\} \;]|$$
$$|[\; x, y: \text{int } \{X = 7 * y \quad \wedge \quad Y = y\}; \text{ S3 } \{X = x \quad \wedge \quad Y = y\} \;]|$$
$$|[\; x, y: \text{int } \{X = 10 * (x - y) \quad \wedge \quad Y = y\}; \text{ S4 } \{X = x \quad \wedge \quad Y = y\} \;]|$$

Remark. In itself it would have been simpler to specify, for S0:

$$|[\; x, y: \text{int } \{y = y\}; \text{ S0 } \{x = 0 \quad \wedge \quad y = Y\} \;]|$$

This specification also expresses neatly that the value of x is zero after execution of S0 (regardless of its initial value: after all, x does not occur in the precondition), and that the value of y has remained unchanged. (Check that the functional specification of S1 could be simplified in a similar way.) In this list such a simplification has deliberately not been carried out, so that the functional specifications are as similar as possible. ∎

The functional specifications given above all have the same pattern, namely:

$$|[\; x, y: \text{int } \{X = E \quad \wedge \quad Y = y\}; \text{ Si } \{X = x \quad \wedge \quad Y = y\} \;]|$$

with E taking the values $0, 88, x + 3, 7 * y$ and $10 * (x - y)$ respectively, and with the name Si.

Our program notation offers the possibility of writing such programs as follows, by means of **assignment statements**:

```
for S0:    x:= 0
for S1:    x:= 88
for S2:    x:= x + 3
for S3:    x:= 7 * y
for S4:    x:= 10 *(x - y)
```

(Pronounce the assignment operator := as 'becomes', that is, 'x becomes zero', 'x becomes eighty-eight', 'x becomes x plus three', 'x becomes seven times y' and 'x becomes ten times opening bracket x minus y closing bracket.')

The postulate of the assignment implies that for each permissible expression E the program x:= E satisfies the functional specification

$$|[\text{x, y: int } \{X = E \land Y = y\}; \text{ x:= } E \{X = x \land Y = y\}]|$$

Any declared variable may be chosen for x; the postulate of the assignment also implies that for any permissible expression E the program y := E satisfies the functional specification

$$|[\text{x, y: int } \{X = x \land Y = E\}; \text{ y:= } E \{X = x \land Y = y\}]|$$

Even more variables could have been declared; the postulate of the assignment then also implies that for any permissible expression E the program x:= E satisfies the functional specification

$$
\begin{aligned}
&|[\text{x, y, z: int} \\
&\quad \{X = E \land Y = y \land Z = z\} \\
&; \text{ x:= } E \\
&\quad \{X = x \land Y = y \land Z = z\} \\
&]|
\end{aligned}
$$

In the above 'permissible expressions' have been mentioned several times without being defined further. However, a definition of which expressions can be regarded as permissible will be postponed. In the meantime, it is sufficient to know that the given examples of expressions are permissible in places where the declaration x, y, z: int is in force. First an example will show how the postulate of the assignment is used to make more particular assertions about a specific assignment statement, such as x:= x + 3; for example, under which precondition x ≥ y will hold after execution. For the sake of clarity, consider this problem in the state space described by x, y, z: int: z then denotes the other variables.

By substituting the permissible expression x + 3 for E in the last formulation of the postulate of the assignment, we get

$$
\begin{aligned}
&|[\text{x, y, z: int} \\
&\quad \{X = x + 3 \land Y = y \land Z = z\}
\end{aligned}
$$

```
;  x:= x + 3
   {X = x   ∧   Y = y   ∧   Z = z}
]|
```

an assertion which holds for all X, Y and Z, in particular for all X, Y and Z which satisfy X ≥ Y. Restricting the application to these cases, we derive

```
|[ x, y, z: int
   {X = x + 3   ∧   Y = y   ∧   Z =z   ∧   X ≥ Y}
;  x:= x + 3
   {X = x   ∧   Y = y   ∧   Z = z   ∧   X ≥ Y}
]|
```

The validity of the postcondition implies x ≥ y, so that the assertion

```
|[ x, y, z: int
   {X = x + 3   ∧   Y = y   ∧   Z = z   ∧   X ≥ Y}
;  x:= x + 3
   {x ≥ y}
]|
```

holds for all X, Y and Z. By rewriting the precondition we may draw the same conclusion for

```
|[ x, y, z: int
   {X = x + 3   ∧   Y = y   ∧   Z = z   ∧   x + 3 ≥ y}
;  x:= x + 3
   {x ≥ y}
]|
```

Since:

(i)   this latter assertion holds for all X, Y and Z;

(ii)   X, Y and Z occur only in the initial part of the precondition

$$X = x + 3 \quad ∧ \quad Y = y \quad ∧ \quad Z = z$$

and this initial part, regarded as an equation in the unknowns X, Y and Z, can be solved for all values of x, y and z;

we can eliminate X, Y and Z by dropping this initial part. We then get:

```
|[ x, y, z: int
   {x + 3 ≥ y}
;  x:= x + 3
   {x ≥ y}
]|
```

In words: the initial validity of $x + 3 \geq y$ justifies the conclusion that, after execution of the assignment statement $x := x + 3$, the relation $x \geq y$ holds. (This conclusion is obviously weaker than what we knew already: it no longer expresses that the execution of $x := x + 3$ leaves the values of y and z intact.)

Here, $x + 3$ was a very particular choice for the right-hand side of the assignment statement. Analogously, we could have derived

$$|[\; x, y, z: \text{int } \{E \geq y\}; \; x := E \; \{x \geq y\} \;]|$$

from the postulate of the assignment for any permissible expression E.

The choice of the postcondition $x \geq y$ was also arbitrary. If we had, for example, chosen $z \cdot (x + 1) \leq (y + 3) \cdot x$, then we would have derived:

$$|[\; x, y, z: \text{int}$$
$$\{z \cdot (E + 1) \leq (y + 3) \cdot E\}$$
$$; \; x := E$$
$$\{z \cdot (x + 1) \leq (y + 3) \cdot x\}$$
$$]|$$

The general pattern for finding the corresponding precondition for the assignment statement $x := E$ and given postcondition R is obviously that we substitute the expression E for x in R, if necessary in brackets. It is common practice to denote this substitution result by R_E^x. With this convention we can sum up our rule as:

$$|[\; x, y, z: \text{int } \{R_E^x\}; \; x := E \; \{R\} \;]|$$

Remark. Application of the rule to the postcondition $\neg R$ yields the assertion:

$$|[\; x, y, z: \text{int } \{\neg R_E^x\}; \; x := E \; \{\neg R\} \;]|$$

From this we see that the initial validity of R_E^x is not only sufficient, but also necessary for $x := E$ to effect a state in which R holds.   ∎

Permissible expressions

A program is a set of instructions that can be executed by a computer. This means that there must be no misunderstanding about what the instructions imply. After reading this far, few people will question that the meaning of the assignment statement

    x:= 2 * x

is that the value of x is doubled. But opinions about the aim of

    x:= x / 2 * 6

are divided (if you ask a large enough number of people). In the Netherlands, where traditionally multiplication comes before division, the view that

    x:= x / (2 * 6)

is meant will prevail. In countries with other traditions, however, it will be assumed that

    x:= (x / 2) * 6

is meant. It is clear that these kinds of ambiguities must be ruled out by exact definitions. This inevitably requires us to define just as exactly *which* expressions have an unambiguous meaning. This section is concerned with this definition. In passing, the most common formalism used for giving such definitions will be introduced, i.e. BNF (Backus–Naur Form, named after John Backus and Peter Naur). BNF became widely known by the way in which it was used in the famous *Algol 60 Report* of January 1960.

Just about the simplest permissible expression is the natural number. BNF will now be used to define what natural numbers look like on paper. Since the notation of natural numbers consists of digits, we shall first define what forms there are for digits. In BNF this is given by the **syntax rule**:

$$\langle digit \rangle ::= 0 \mid 1 \mid 2 \mid 3 \mid 4 \mid 5 \mid 6 \mid 7 \mid 8 \mid 9$$

To the left of the sign ::= (pronounced 'is defined as') is the name of the syntactic unit to be defined, placed in angle brackets; to the right of the ::= sign are the forms of the syntactic unit, separated by a vertical mark, | (pronounced 'or'). The rule states which ten characters are digits and, moreover, that if later on we come across $\langle digit \rangle$ in a syntactic formula, this can denote any one of these ten characters.

Remark. The order in which alternative forms are listed in a syntax rule is irrelevant. We could have defined the syntactic unit *digit* just as well by:

$$\langle digit \rangle ::= 9 \mid 8 \mid 7 \mid 6 \mid 5 \mid 4 \mid 3 \mid 2 \mid 1 \mid 0 \qquad \blacksquare$$

Now we have the tool to define, if we should want to, which character sequences belong to the syntactic unit *number under thousand*:

$\langle number\ under\ thousand \rangle$
$\quad ::= \langle digit \rangle$
$\quad \mid \langle digit \rangle \langle digit \rangle$
$\quad \mid \langle digit \rangle \langle digit \rangle \langle digit \rangle$

The above definition tells us that a *number under thousand* has three alternative forms: a single digit, two digits in a row, or a sequence of three digits. It would be a dismal writing lesson to write out in this way the forms of *number under billion*. It would be hopeless to write in this way the forms of a natural number. In BNF the syntactic unit of a natural number is given by:

$\langle natural\ number \rangle$
$\quad ::= \langle digit \rangle$
$\quad \mid \langle digit \rangle \langle natural\ number \rangle$

This is a **recursive definition**: the syntactic unit defined occurs in its own definition (namely in the second alternative)! The first confrontation with a recursive definition usually sends a shiver down one's spine: one cannot help thinking of the snake that bites its own tail and begins to eat itself, continuing until nothing is left. Having overcome this shiver, however, people learn to appreciate recursive definitions; without them we would not be able to define a syntactic unit with an unlimited number of forms.

On thinking it over, this definition of (the syntax of) *natural number* is not as uncanny as it may seem at first sight, thanks to the presence of the first alternative. In the definition of *digit*, the first alternative presents us with ten forms of a natural number (and by this the first alternative is, as it were, exhausted). With these ten forms as possible substitutes for *natural number* in the second alternative, 100 new forms are yielded, with these 100 as possible substitutes in the second alternative we get 1000 new forms, etc.

Remark. The syntax rule

⟨ *natural number* ⟩
    ::= ⟨ *digit* ⟩
        | ⟨ *natural number* ⟩ ⟨ *digit* ⟩

is equivalent to the one given before. Both define the set of finite, non-empty sequences of digits.   ∎

In an analogous way to our definition of *digit* we define:

⟨ *letter* ⟩ ::= a | b | c | d | e | f | g | h | i | j | k | l | m
                n | o | p | q | r | s | t | u | v | w | x | y | z
                A | B | C | D | E | F | G | H | I | J | K | L | M
                N | O | P | Q | R | S | T | U | V | W | X | Y | Z

Remark. With this it has been defined that an alphabet of 52 different characters will be used. Note that:

- the digit 0 and the letters o and O are different characters;
- the digit 1 and the letters l and I are different characters;
- the digit 9 and the letter g are different characters.

Furthermore, since the order of the alternatives in a syntax rule has no meaning, the 52 letters are not combined as pairs, and therefore the letter sequence *dog* has nothing to do with the letter sequences *Dog* or *DOG*.   ∎

These examples have introduced local variables, for instance by the declaration

    x, y, z: int

introducing their 'names' (x, y and z respectively) in passing. Just as the forms of a natural number have been defined, those of a name will now be defined.

Remark. In the English literature the standard term for *name* is 'identifier'. We shall stick to the syntax of Algol 60 identifiers for names.   ■

$$\langle name \rangle ::= \langle letter \rangle$$
$$| \ \langle name \rangle \ \langle letter \rangle$$
$$| \ \langle name \rangle \ \langle digit \rangle$$

EXERCISE

Check that there are 199 888 different names of three characters.

Now we are ready for the definition of the syntax of expressions which are permissible. At this stage we shall confine ourselves to the syntactic unit called **integer expression**; the syntax describes how integer expressions are constructed from:

- names and natural numbers;
- additive operators;
- multiplicative operators;
- pairs of brackets.

Remarks. At this stage the text is deliberately confined to a modest syntax for integer expressions. Later this will be expanded a little.   ■

$$\langle integer \ expression \rangle$$
$$::= \langle intterm \rangle$$
$$| \ \langle addop \rangle \ \langle intterm \rangle$$
$$| \ \langle integer \ expression \rangle \ \langle addop \rangle \ \langle intterm \rangle$$

This syntax rule tells us that an integer expression is a sequence in which specimens of the syntax unit *addop* and specimens of the syntax unit *intterm* alternate, and which ends with a (specimen of the syntax unit) *intterm*. All we have to do now is to state what an *addop* and an *intterm* may lok like. For the former this is more simple than it is for the latter.

$$\langle addop \rangle ::= + \mid -$$

$$\langle intterm \rangle$$
$$::= \langle intfactor \rangle$$
$$\mid \langle intterm \rangle \langle multop \rangle \langle intfactor \rangle$$

This completes the definition of *addop*: a plus sign or a minus sign. The following syntax rule tells us that an *intterm* consists of one or more specimens of the syntactic unit *intfactor*, separated by a specimen of the syntactic unit *multop*. And all we have to do now is to state what a *multop* and an *intfactor* may look like; here again this is simpler for the former than it is for the latter:

$$\langle multop \rangle ::= * \mid / \mid \mathbf{div} \mid \mathbf{mod}$$

$$\langle intfactor \rangle$$
$$::= \langle natural\ number \rangle$$
$$\mid \langle name \rangle$$
$$\mid (\langle integer\ expression \rangle)$$

This completes the syntactic definition of the integer expression. Analysis of an example will show that

$$- ab - x \underline{\mathrm{mod}}\ 3 + 8 *(y + 1)$$

is an integer expression.

This holds because:

(0)	$- ab - x \underline{\mathrm{mod}}\ 3$ is an *integer* expression
(1)	$+$ is an *addop* (self-evident)
(2)	$8 *(y + 1)$ is an *intterm*

Assertion (0) holds because:

(0.0)	$- ab$ is an *integer* expression
(0.1)	$-$ is an *addop* (self-evident)
(0.2)	$x \underline{\mathrm{mod}}\ 3$ is an *intterm*

Assertion (0.0) holds because:

(0.0.0)	$-$ is an addop (self-evident)
(0.0.1)	ab is an *intterm*

Assertion (0.0.1) holds because:

(0.0.1.0)   ab is an *intfactor*

Assertion (0.0.1.0) holds because:

(0.0.1.0.0)   ab is a *name*

Assertion (0.0.1.0.0) holds because:

(0.0.1.0.0.0)   a is a *name*
(0.0.1.0.0.1)   b is a *letter* (self-evident)

Assertion (0.0.1.0.0.0) holds because:

(0.0.1.0.0.0.0) a is a *letter* (self-evident)

Thus assertion (0.0) is proved; (0.1) is self-evident, and (0.2) holds because:

(0.2.0)   x is an *intterm*
(0.2.1)   mod is a *multop* (self-evident)
(0.2.2)   3 is an *intfactor*

Assertion (0.2.0) holds because:

(0.2.0.0)   x is an *intfactor*

Assertion (0.2.0.0) holds because:

(0.2.0.0.0)   x is a *name*

Assertion (0.2.0.0.0) holds because:

(0.2.0.0.0.0)   x is a *letter* (self-evident)

Thus assertion (0.2.0) is proved; (0.2.1) is self-evident, and (0.2.2) holds because:

(0.2.2.0)   3 is a *natural number*

Assertion (0.2.2.0) holds because:

(0.2.2.0.0)   3 is a *digit* (self-evident)

With this (0.2.2) is proved, and thus (0.2), and thus (0.2), and thus (0); (1) is self-evident and the proof of (2) is left to the reader.

We do not suggest that he or she produce such a long-winded proof as this for (0), but that the reader should be aware of each appeal to formal syntax. The analysis is given in such small steps in order that: (1) the reader can imagine that this can be done by a mechanism; and (2) the reader may appreciate the fact that a formal definition of the syntax is essential for this. (The development and first implementation of FORTRAN in the mid-1950s took 100 times more man-years than the first implementation of Algol 60 in 1960. The two projects differed enough to warrant some caution in interpreting this factor of 100; however, they were similar enough to tend to explain this factor, among other things, by the circumstance that there was no formal definition of FORTRAN.)

Furthermore, this syntax of integer expressions makes it explicity clear that additive operators are 'left-associative'; that is, an integer expression like $-$ a $-$ b $+$ c, for example, is an integer expression only in the analysis

((– a) – b) + c

and that interpretations such as

(– a) – (b + c)   and   –(a – (b + c)

are not permitted. So the syntax for integer expressions does more than merely define what sequences of symbols are integer expressions: it also indicates how the expression must be interpreted; that is, which constants and which intermediary results must be the operands of which operators when the expression is being computed.

EXERCISE

Determine why 2k + 1is not a syntactically correct integer expression.

Remark. The multiplicative operators are also defined left-associatively and no priority has been assigned to multiplication over division: m / 2 * h is thus short for (m / 2)* h and *not* for m /(2 * h). If the latter is intended, the brackets cannot be left out. The advice not to be too stingy with pairs of brackets has a much wider application, however. There is often no consensus about what can be left out without a change of meaning. ■

It only remains for us now to define the operators. If the additive operators occur as binary operators, the addition is denoted by + and the subtraction by −, and if they occur as a unary operator – that is, as the first symbol of an integer expression – the + has no effect and the − denotes a change of sign. The reader presumably knows what is meant by addition, subtraction and change of sign.

The remaining multiplicative operators, /, div and mod are **partial operators**, that is x / y, x div y and x mod y are not defined for all pairs of integer values (x, y).

x / y denotes the quotient of x and y, which naturally is defined only if y ≠ 0; furthermore, in using x / y, we agree to confine ourselves to those situations in which x is an integer number of times y.

For x div y and x mod y there is only the restriction y ≠ 0: x div y = q and x mod y = r, where integer q and r satisfy:

$$x = q \cdot y + r \wedge 0 \leq r < abs(y)$$

Note that:

$$x \; \underline{mod} \; y = x \; \underline{mod} \, (- \, y)$$
$$(- \, x) \underline{div} \; y \neq - \, x \; \underline{div} \; y, \text{ unless } x \; \underline{mod} \; y = 0$$
$$(x + y) \underline{mod} \; y = x \; \underline{mod} \; y$$
$$(x + y) \underline{div} \; y = 1 + x \; \underline{div} \; y$$

This completes, for now, the description of what we had indicated as permissible expressions.

Concatenation of statements

Until now we have only come across the assignment statement in the form x := E, and so far, the programs we can write are rather limited for two reasons. Firstly, the change of state they can effect is restricted to the change of the value of one variable of the state space; secondly, its new value is restricted to what we can express by means of a permissible expression. We shall now see how the first restriction is overcome.

In all places where we can write a statement, we can also write a *statement list*

> ⟨*statement list*⟩
> ::= ⟨*statement*⟩
> | ⟨*statement list*⟩ ⟨*statement*⟩

that is, a list of one or more statements, in the latter case connected by the semicolon. The semicolon, which is written between two consecutive statements, connects those two statements in the sense that execution of the left-hand statement must be followed by that of the right-hand statement, and that the postcondition of the left-hand statement is identified as the precondition of the right-hand statement.

At the end of our discussion about the assignment statement (page 22) the general structure of assertions about a single assignment statement was given as:

$$|[\ x, \ y, \ z: \ \text{int} \ \{Q\}; \ x := E0 \ \{R\} \ ]|$$

This means that if, before the execution of x := E0, Q is satisfied, then after execution of x := E0 the state satisfies R; this assertion is true if Q equals R_{E0}^{x}, i.e. the condition R in which the expression E0 is substituted for x – in brackets if necessary, but we shall no longer repeat this every time.

With $P = Q_{E1}^{Y}$

$$|[\; x, y, z: \text{int } \{P\}; \; y := E1; \; x := E0 \; \{R\} \;]|$$

is also a correct assertion, this time about the assignment statement $y := E1$. The postulate about concatenation implies that these two assertions may be combined to

$$|[\; x, y, z: \text{int } \{P\}; \; y := E1 \; \{Q\}; \; x := E0 \; \{R\} \;]|$$

or, if we eliminate Q by suppressing it, to the assertion about $y := E1; \; x := E0$:

$$|[\; x, y, z: \text{int } \{P\}; \; y := E1; \; x := E0 \; \{R\} \;]|$$

Now we can also check what assertions we can make if we switch the two statements, that is, assertions of the form:

$$|[\; x, y, z: \text{int } \{P'\}; \; x := E0; \; y := E1 \; \{R\} \;]|$$

Working from right to left, we first form $Q' = R^Y_{E1}$ and then $P' = Q'^X_{E0}$. In general, $P \neq P'$ – namely if x occurs in $E1$, or y in $E0$. In other words, concatenation of statements is generally *not* commutative.

As an example we shall derive P, so that the assertion

$$
\begin{aligned}
&|[\; x, y, z: \text{int } \{P\} \\
&\quad ; \; x := x + y; \; y := x - y; \; x := x - y \\
&\qquad \{x = X \; \wedge \; y = Y \; \wedge \; z = Z\} \\
&\quad]|
\end{aligned}
$$

holds.

To begin with we introduce the suppressed intermediary conditions – two by now:

$$
\begin{aligned}
&|[\; x, y, z: \text{int } \{P\} \\
&\quad ; \; x := x + y \; \{Q1\} \\
&\quad ; \; y := x - y \; \{Q0\} \\
&\quad ; \; x := x - y \\
&\qquad \{x = X \; \wedge \; y = Y \; \wedge \; z = Z\} \\
&\quad]|
\end{aligned}
$$

Working back to front, by substituting $x - y$ for x we get:

$$Q0: \quad x - y = X \; \wedge \; y = Y \; \wedge \; z = Z$$

Substituting y by $x - y$ in this, we get

$$Q1: \quad x - (x - y) = X \; \wedge \; x - y = Y \; \wedge \; z = Z$$

and after simplification

Q1:   y = X   ∧   x − y = Y   ∧   z = Z

Substituting x by x + y in this, we get

P: y = X   ∧   (x + y) − y = Y   ∧   z = Z

and after simplification

P: y = X   ∧   x = Y   ∧   z = Z

If we compare P with the postcondition, we see that the 'continued concatenation'

x:= x + y; y:= x − y; x:= x − y

swaps the values of x and y and leaves all other variables undisturbed.

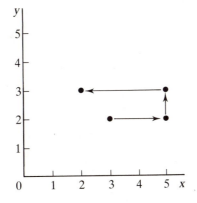

Figure 4

In Figure 4, showing a projection of the state space on the plane x, y, the path for the special case X = 2   ∧   Y = 3 is indicated. The figure is given only as an illustration of the fact that the statement concatenation enables us to construct programs that effect the desired change of state not at one go, but in a number of consecutive steps. In this metaphor the computation becomes a path through the state space which leads from the starting point to the end point. We shall see later that in actual practice these paths tend to be traversed in a great many steps.

Figure 4 is *only* an illustration of the metaphor. In programming practice such figures are never drawn. They would have the practical drawback of becoming terribly complicated and the fundamental drawback of referring only to a very specific case (in this case $X = 2 \quad \wedge \quad Y = 3$).

Remark. The continued concatenation above was produced only for reasons of illustration. Later we shall come across more realistic solutions to exchange the values of two variables.   ∎

The alternative statement

In the preceding section we saw that for a given program the path through the state space depends on the initial state, but as long as we have only assignment statements and their concatenation at our disposal, the same series of statements will always be executed, independently of the initial state. We shall now show that for a given program the initial state can also determine *which* statements will be executed. A study of the functional specification of the program largest will reveal the need for this greater flexibility:

```
|[ x, y, z: int {x = X  ∧  y = Y}
 ; largest {x = X  ∧  y = Y  ∧  z = max(x, y)}
 ]|
```

The problem would be trivial if max(x, y) were among the permissible expressions, since z := max(x, y) would then satisfy the functional specification of largest. But since max(x, y) is not among the permissible expressions, we must do something else.

Remark. There are programming languages that allow the programmer to add max(x, y) to the set of permissible expressions. However, the addition requires a solution to the problem of how to write a program that satisfies the functional specification of largest in terms of the expressions already permissible. ∎

To begin with, we observe that with the postcondition for largest we can derive, by means of the postulate of the assignment statement for z := x:

```
|[ x, y, z: int {x = X  ∧  y = Y  ∧  x = max(x, y)}
 ; z:= x {x = X  ∧  y = Y  ∧  z = max(x, y)}
 ]|
```

Furthermore, we observe that for x and y

$$(x = max(x, y)) = (x \geq y)$$

i.e. x = max(x,y) and x ≥ y are either both true or both false; this equality enables us to eliminate the 'non-permissible' expression max(x, y) from the precondition:

```
|[ x, y, z: int {x = X  ∧  y = Y  ∧  x ≥ y}
; z:= x {x = X  ∧  y = Y  ∧  z = max(x, y)}
]|
```

In the same way we derive:

```
|[ x, y, z: int {x = X  ∧  y = Y  ∧  y ≥ x}
; z:= y {x = X  ∧  y = Y  ∧  z = max(x, y)}
]|
```

From the last term of the initial state we can see that in some initial states, namely if x ≥ y, the assignment z:=x brings about the desired effect, and that in (largely) other initial states, namely if y ≥ x, the assignment statement z := y does so. Since x ≥ y ∨ y ≥ x always holds, both assignment statements together cover all cases, and it would be useful to combine them, leaving the choice at execution up to the initial state. This can be done by means of the **alternative statement**:

```
|[ x, y, z: int {x = X  ∧  y = Y}
; if  x ≥ y → z:= x ◻  y  ≥ x → z:= y fi
  {x = X  ∧  y = Y  ∧  z = max(x, y)}
]|
```

This form of combination is not confined to two programs: it can be done for any finite number. The general plan of the case of three, again with a state space spanned by x, y and z, is the postulate of the alternative statement.
Together the three assertions

```
|[ x, y, z: int {P  ∧  B0}; S0 {R} ]|
|[ x, y, z: int {P  ∧  B1}; S1 {R} ]|
|[ x, y, z: int {P  ∧  B2}; S2 {R} ]|
```

justify the assertion:

```
|[ x, y, z: int {P  ∧  (B0  ∨  B1  ∨  B2)}
;   if  B0 → S0
    ◻  B1 → S1
```

```
     ▯   B2 → S2
     fi  {R}
]|
```

Remark. In this example direct application of the rule would have yielded the precondition

$$\{x = X \quad \wedge \quad y = Y \quad \wedge \quad (x \geq y \quad \vee \quad y \geq x)\}$$

but because, as observed, the last term always holds, it can be left out without a change of meaning.   ■

First we shall expand our syntax correspondingly:

⟨ *statement* ⟩
       ::= *skip*
         | ⟨ *assignment statement* ⟩
         | ⟨ *alternative statement* ⟩

⟨ *alternative statement* ⟩
       ::= **if** ⟨ *guarded command set* ⟩ **fi**

⟨ *guarded command set* ⟩
       ::= ⟨ *guarded command* ⟩
         | ⟨ *guarded command set* ⟩ ▯ ⟨ *guarded command* ⟩

⟨ *guarded command* ⟩
       ::= ⟨ *guard* ⟩ → ⟨ *statement list* ⟩

A guard is a so-called **Boolean expression**; the exact definition of permitted Boolean expressions is postponed for the present.

It follows from the postulate of the alternative statement that the order in which the *guarded commands* are listed within the pair of brackets **if** . . . **fi** is irrelevant. (It is for this reason that the syntactic unit is called *guarded command set* and not *guarded command list*.)

EXERCISE

Derive from the postulate of the alternative statement the fact that, although permitted, it is useless to have a specific guarded command occur more than once in a guarded command set.

Operationally, a guarded command of the form $B \rightarrow S$ implies that the statement list S will be executed only in those initial states in which guard B holds.

Operationally, the alternative statement implies that exactly one of the guarded commands is selected for execution, namely one whose guard is originally *true*. If all guards are *false* in the initial state of an alternative statement, this is considered a programming error (which in any reasonable implication results in an immediate interruption of the execution of the program). Therefore it is the programmer's obligation to demonstrate that, just before any alternative statement, at least one of the guards holds. (In the example for largest this obligation was trivial.) A consequence of all this is that there is little use for alternative statements with only one guarded command.

We point out that in those cases in which *more* than one guard holds, it is completely open which statement list with a valid guard will be selected for execution. With the text for largest

$$\text{if } x \geq y \rightarrow z := x \ \square \ y \geq x \rightarrow z := y \text{ fi}$$

and initial state $x = 7 \ \wedge \ y = 7$, both guards hold. It does not matter whether $z = 7$ is produced by $z := x$ or by $z := y$.

If there is the possibility of a choice, the fact that this choice is left completely free because the guards are not mutually exclusive, introduces **non-determinism**. In the case of non-determinism the path through the state space, and thus the final state, need no longer be uniquely determined by the initial state, as is illustrated by the statement whose specification expresses that its execution does or does not change the sign of x:

```
|[ x: int
   {x = X}
 ; if true → x := - x  ☐  true → skip fi
   {abs(x) = abs(X)}
]|
```

There is never any need to write a non-deterministic program. It so happens that from a non-deterministic program that satisfies a particular specification a deterministic program satisfying the same specification can always be derived.

Let the functional specification of statement S be given by precondition P and postcondition Q, or more precisely

$$|[x, y, z: \text{int } \{P\}; S \{Q\}]|$$

Let this specification be demonstrably satisfied by an S of the form

$$\text{if } B0 \rightarrow S0 \ \square \ B1 \rightarrow S1 \text{ fi}$$

Because of the postulate of the alternative statement, this implies the correctness of the following assertions:

$$P \Rightarrow (B0 \lor B1)$$
$$|[x, y, z: int \{P \land B0\}; S0 \{Q\}]|$$
$$|[x, y, z: int \{P \land B1\}; S1 \{Q\}]|$$

From this, however, it follows that (in order)

$$P \Rightarrow (B0 \lor (B1 \land \neg B0))$$
$$|[x, y, z: int \{P \land B0\}; S0 \{Q\}]|$$
$$|[x, y, z: int \{P \land B1 \land \neg B0\}; S1 \{Q\}]|$$

from which, on the basis of the postulate of the alternative statement, we may conclude that for S we may also have chosen

$$\underline{if}\ B0 \to S0\ [\!]\ B1 \land \neg B0 \to S1\ \underline{fi}$$

i.e. the guard of one guarded command can freely be strengthened by the additional restriction that the other guarded command does not qualify for execution. But now we have an alternative statement in which the guards exclude each other and which is thus deterministic. Expelling non-determinism in this way from the solution we found for largest leads to the deterministic solutions

$$\underline{if}\ x \geq y \to z := x\ [\!]\ y > x \to z := y\ \underline{fi}$$

and

$$\underline{if}\ x > y \to z := x\ [\!]\ y \geq x \to z := y\ \underline{fi}$$

EXERCISE

Show that the following alternative statement satisfies the specification of largest:

```
if  x > y → z := x
 [] x = y → z := (x + y)/2
 [] x < y → z := y
fi
```

Although the need to design non-deterministic programs will not occur in this book, it is highly desirable to learn how to reason about non-deterministic programs. During the design process we must be able to reason about half-finished programs, in which all kinds of decisions about details have not yet been made: such a half-finished program is often in the form of a non-deterministic program.

Permissible Boolean expressions

This section gives the syntax for Boolean expressions that may function as guards. The syntax will again be given in BNF. Its construction resembles that of the integer expression – the way in which brackets are introduced, for example, is quite analogous; the abundance of operators, however, makes it a little more complicated.

⟨ *Boolean expression* ⟩
    ::= ⟨ *disjunction* ⟩
    | ⟨ *disjunction* ⟩ ≡ ⟨ *disjunction* ⟩
    | ⟨ *disjunction* ⟩ ≢ ⟨ *disjunction* ⟩

⟨ *disjunction* ⟩
    ::= ⟨ *conjunction* ⟩
    | ⟨ *disjunction* ⟩ ∨ ⟨ *conjunction* ⟩
    | ⟨ *disjunction* ⟩ **cor** ⟨ *conjunction* ⟩

⟨ *conjunction* ⟩
    ::= ⟨ *Boolean term* ⟩
    | ⟨ *conjunction* ⟩ ∧ ⟨ *Boolean term* ⟩
    | ⟨ *conjunction* ⟩ **cand** ⟨ *Boolean term* ⟩

⟨ *Boolean term* ⟩
    ::= ⟨ *Boolean primary* ⟩
    | ¬ ⟨ *Boolean primary* ⟩

⟨ *Boolean primary* ⟩
    ::= *true*
    | *false*
    | ⟨ *name* ⟩
    | ⟨ *integer expression* ⟩ ⟨ *relop* ⟩ ⟨ *integer expression* ⟩
    | (⟨ *Boolean expression* ⟩)

⟨ *relop* ⟩ ::= < | ≦ | > | ≧ | = | ≠

If so desired, we may write: **and** for $\wedge$, **or** for $\vee$, and **not** for $\neg$. (This can have its advantages, especially when using a typewriter.)

The operators **cand** and **cor** stand for 'conditional and' and 'conditional or'. If both operands a and b are defined, we have

$$a \textbf{ cand } b \equiv a \wedge b$$

and

$$a \textbf{ cor } b \equiv a \vee b$$

In contrast to the operators $\wedge$ and $\vee$, which are defined only if both operands are defined,

$$false \textbf{ cand } b \equiv false$$

and

$$true \textbf{ cor } b \equiv true$$

are defined also in those cases in which b is undefined. Thus, in contrast to $\wedge$ and $\vee$, **cand** and **cor** are not commutative. Provided that we do not change the order of the operands, de Morgan's Law does hold for them, that is:

$$\neg(a \textbf{ cand } b) \equiv (\neg a)\textbf{cor}(\neg b)$$

Note that $a \wedge b \vee c$ can be analysed in one way only, that is, as the disjunction of $a \wedge b$ and c. (The attempt to analyse it to the conjunction of a and $b \vee c$ fails because according to the syntax the right-hand operand of $\wedge$ must be a Boolean term, and $b \vee c$ does not have the appearance of a Boolean term.) So the syntax expresses the common convention that $\wedge$ has a higher priority ('greater binding power') than $\vee$. It is generally preferred not to stint on pairs of brackets. (Note that we may also have written

$$\neg(a \textbf{ cand } b) \equiv \neg a \textbf{ cor } \neg b$$

instead of the above representation of de Morgan's Law.) It would not be wise to be too sparing with brackets on the grounds of the greater binding power of $\wedge$ over $\vee$ if this interferes with the symmetry, as in the formulation of the theorem that for all Boolean p, q and r it holds that:

$$(p \vee q) \wedge (q \vee r) \wedge (r \vee p) \equiv$$
$$(p \wedge q) \vee (q \wedge r) \vee (r \wedge p)$$

EXERCISE

Prove the theorem just given.

Remark. Provided that the type of all variables and constants is fixed unambiguously – and in our case this will be shown to be so later – there is no ambiguity introduced when the Boolean equality $\equiv$ is denoted by the symbol = also used for the equality of integers. If, for example, it is fixed unambiguously that where it says

$$x = y = b$$

x and y denote integer values and b a Boolean value, this can only be interpreted as

$$(x = y) \equiv b$$

In this field there are no generally accepted conventions, and in this book we shall overcome this lack of consensus by not using brackets too sparingly, as said before, and by using, perhaps superfluously, the special symbol $\equiv$ for the Boolean equality. The price is not heavy, since we shall rarely come across very complicated Boolean expressions. ■

Analogously to variables 'of the type *integer*', we can also declare variables 'of the type Boolean': they have only two possible values, called *true* and *false*, respectively. We have the following syntax for declarations:

⟨*declaration*⟩ ::= ⟨*name list*⟩ : ⟨*type*⟩
⟨*name list*⟩ ::= ⟨*name*⟩
　　　　　| ⟨*name list*⟩ , ⟨*name*⟩
⟨*type*⟩ ::= *int* | *bool*
⟨*declaration list*⟩
　　　::= ⟨*declaration*⟩
　　　| ⟨*declaration list*⟩ ; ⟨*declaration*⟩

The names in the *name list* are separated by commas and successive declarations are separated (or connected!) by semicolons. So the description of a state space can, for example, begin with

|[x, t: int; b: bool

Analogously to the assignment of the type *integer*, we also have the assignment of the type *Boolean*, for example,

```
b := x ≥ y
```

execution of which determines the new value of b, according to whether $x \geq y$ or not.

Remark. For the first 15 years, program execution was understood as a combination of 'the computation of numbers' and 'the testing of conditions'. While the result of such a (numerical) computation was formed and stored for later use in the register or memory, the result of the test of a condition was used immediately (as in an alternative statement) to influence the further execution of the computation. One merit of Algol 60 was that by introducing variables of the type *Boolean*, it was made clear that the testing of a condition could be better understood as a computation – not as the computation of a number but as the computation of a 'truth value'. This generalization of the idea of computation is a very important contribution: the proof of a theorem can now be regarded as the demonstration that the computation of a proposition yields the value *true*. Although we shall only come across a modest number of variables of the type *Boolean* in our programs, the type *Boolean* should not be missing from any introduction to programming. The old-fashioned habit, still found in electrical engineering, of identifying the values *true* and *false* by the integers 1 and 0 respectively must not be imitated: it only leads to confusion. ∎

The repetitive statement

Something quite essential is still missing from our stock of possibilities for program construction. As long as we had only concatenation, the execution of a program consisted of as many statements as we had listed. The effect of the alternative statement is that statements, although written down, may not be executed, because another alternative is chosen.

There are, however, computation jobs which are intrinsically very laborious. (They are the very jobs from which the computer derives its right to exist! It is exactly these jobs that justify the great speed of arithmetic units and memories.) These computation jobs are so very laborious because the desired change of state can be effected only by a very long path, consisting of a great many small steps.

The reader should realize that machines that execute a million assignments in a few seconds are not at all unusual. It is obvious that programming such a machine would be an impossible task, if we first had to write a million statements, only to keep it busy for a few seconds. It must be possible to write short programs to which long computations correspond; without this possibility these long computation processes could not be realized.

Let us go back to the formal specification of euclid:

```
|[ x, y: int
    {X = gcd(x, y)   ∧   x > 0   ∧   y > 0}

; euclid
    {x = X}   ∧   y = X}
]|
```

Since $gcd(X, X) = X$ and $X > 0$, the precondition still holds in the final state; moreover, $x = y$ in the final state. With P defined as

$$P: \quad X = gcd(x, y) \quad \wedge \quad x > 0 \quad \wedge \quad y > 0$$

we can also specify euclid by

|[x, y: int {P}; euclid {P   ∧   x = y}]|

because, conversely, the original postcondition follows from P   ∧   x = y. (Check this.) This last functional specification puts the task of euclid in a different light: euclid must effect x = y without disrupting the validity of P. If we cannot do it in one go, we shall be satisfied if, without disrupting P, we can take a step in the right direction. This step can then be repeated until our goal x = y is achieved. If the goal x = y is not achieved, either x > y holds or y > x. Since the gcd of two numbers equals that of one of the two and their difference, the following two statements hold:

|[x, y: int {P   ∧   x > y}; x := x − y {P}]|
|[x, y: int {P   ∧   y > x}; y := y − x {P}]| .

A solution for euclid would now be:

do x > y → x:= x − y
❒ y > x → y:= y − x
od

Again the order in which the guarded commands are listed in the pair of brackets do . . . od is irrelevant. Operationally, a guarded command of the form B → S implies that the statement list S will be executed only in those initial states for which guard B holds.

The pair of brackets do . . . od forms a **repetitive statement**. A repetitive statement terminates only in states in which none of its guards holds. Operationally, the execution of a repetitive statement implies the following.

If all guards are found *false*, further execution of the repetitive statement is reduced to a skip; otherwise a guarded command, of which the guard is *true*, is executed, after which this process is repeated. (Hence the name repetitive statement.)

Thus the repetitive statement do B → S od is, for example, equivalent to the longer program:

if ¬B → skip
❒ B → S; do B → S od
fi

Remark. This equivalence can be used for the definition of do B → S od . ∎

Suppose that euclid is executed in the initial state $(x, y) = (8, 6)$. The first guard holds, and execution of $x := x - y$ leads to the state $(2, 6)$; then the second guard holds, and execution of $y := y - x$ leads to $(2, 4)$; again the second guard holds and execution of $y := y - x$ leads to $(2, 2)$; since both guards are now *false*, this completes the execution of the repetitive statement.

The corresponding extension of our syntax is:

⟨*statement*⟩ ::= *skip*
| ⟨*assignment statement*⟩
| ⟨*alternative statement*⟩
| ⟨*repetitive statement*⟩

⟨*repetitive statement*⟩
::= **do** ⟨*guarded command set*⟩ **od**

We shall formulate the postulate of the repetitive statement for the case of two guarded commands (leaving the generalization more or less to the reader).

Together, the assertions

|[x, y, z: int {P ∧ B0}; S0 {P}]|
|[x, y, z: int {P ∧ B1}; S1 {P}]|

justify the assertion

```
|[ x, y, z: int
    {P}
  ; do B0 → S0
      ▯ B1 → S1
    od
    {P  ∧  ¬B0  ∧  ¬B1}
  ]|
```

provided that the repetitive statement terminates. (We shall return to this extra condition later.) Appealing to the postulate of the repetitive statement, the predicate, denoted here by P, is called the **invariant**.

We shall now extend the program euclid, which computes the gcd of two positive numbers, to the program euclidplus, which also computes their lowest common multiple (lcm). With the same P as before:

P: $X = gcd(x, y) ∧ x > 0 ∧ y > 0$

the *tentative* (it will become clear later why it is tentative) functional specification of euclidplus is:

```
|[ x, y, u, v: int
    {P ∧ Y = lcm (x, y)}
  ; euclidplus
    {x = X ∧ y = Y}
  ]|
```

We define **Q** by

Q: P ∧ x·u + y·v = 2·X·Y

and to start with we find

(0) |[x, y, u, v: int
           {P ∧ Y = lcm (x, y)}
         ; u:= y; v:= x
           {Q}
         ]|

which is based on the theorem that for positive x and y

gcd(x, y)·lcm(x, y) = x·y

Furthermore, we find

(1) |[x, y, u, v: int
           {Q ∧ x > y}
         ; x:= x − y; v:= v + u
           {Q}
         ]|

because x:= x − y; v:= v + u (check this!) does not change the value of the sum x·u + y·v. So for reasons of symmetry we also have

(2) |[x, y, u, v: int
           {Q ∧ y > x}
         ; y:= y − x; u:= u + v
           {Q}
         ]|

and according to the postulate of the repetitive statement we can combine (1) and (2), provided they terminate, to

(3) |[x, y, u, v: int {Q}
         ; do x > y → x:= x − y; v:= v + u
           ▯ y > x → y:= y − x; u:= u + v
           od {Q ∧ x = y}
         ]|

because $(\neg x > y \land \neg y > x) \equiv (x = y)$.

Since P $\land$ x = y justifies the conclusion x = X $\land$ y = X, Q $\land$ x = y justifies the conclusion X·(u + v) = 2·X·Y or Y = (u + v)/2, from which we may conclude

(4) |[x, y, u, v: int
              {Q $\land$ x = y}
            ; y:= (u + v)/ 2
              {x = X $\land$ y = Y}
            ]|

Combination of (0), (3) and (4) then yields:

    |[x, y, u, v: int {P $\land$ lcm (x, y) = Y}
    ; u:= y; v:= x {Q}
    ; do x > y → x:= x − y; v:= v + u
       ▯ y > x → y:= y − x; u:= u + v
       od {Q $\land$ x = y}
    ; y:= (u + v)/ 2 {x = X $\land$ y = Y}
    ]|

A comparison of the above assertion with the tentative specification of euclidplus tells us that

    u:= y; v:= x
    ; do x > y → x:= x − y; v:= v + u
       ▯ y > x → y:= y − x; u:= u + v
       od; y:= (u + v)/ 2

satisfies the tentative specification of euclidplus.

We have produced our solution for euclidplus for two altogether different reasons. Firstly, it illustrates nicely the power of the postulate of the repetitive statement: without knowledge of the invariant Q, it is not easy to see that in our last program, after termination of the repetition, the average of u and v equals the lowest common multiple of the initial values of x and y. Secondly, the tentative functional specification of euclidplus shows an anomaly. The first line is

    |[x, y, u, v: int

but (see P) variables u and v appear neither in the precondition nor in the postcondition of the functional specification of euclidplus! We may therefore be inclined to say that they should not appear at all in the functional specification of euclidplus, i.e. the definitive functional specification should be

```
|[ x, y: int
   {P ∧ Y = lcm (x, y)}
 ; euclidplus
   {x = X ∧ y = Y}
 ]|
```

An intermezzo about inner blocks

So far we have only come across the brackets |[and]| as opening and closing symbols of functional specifications. Their function was to denote the textual boundaries within whose range the names of the variables used to span the state space in which the functional specification must be understood were valid.

We now introduce the same pair of brackets and the declaration of local variables as a part not of the functional specification but of *program texts*.

For this we extend our syntax:

⟨*statement*⟩ ::= *skip*
      | ⟨*assignment statement*⟩
      | ⟨*alternative statement*⟩
      | ⟨*repetitive statement*⟩
      | ⟨*inner block*⟩

⟨*inner block*⟩
      ::= |[⟨*declaration list*⟩ ; ⟨*statement list*⟩]|

The program that satisfies the definitive functional specification of euclidplus has the form of an inner block and appears as follows:

```
|[ u, v: int
 ; u:= y; v:= x
 ; do x > y  →  x:= x − y; v:= v + u
    ◻ y > x  →  y:= y − x; u:= u + v
   od
 ; y:= (u + v)/ 2
 ]|
```

The inner block has a very clear operational meaning. If it is activated – we could also say 'on entering it' – the state space holding outside it is extended with the variables which are declared in the opening of the inner block; the statements following the declaration are executed in the state space thus extended. The completion of the execution of the inner block consists of deleting the temporary extension of the state space again.

In our example the two-dimensional state space (with coordinates x and y) is extended to a four-dimensional one (namely with u and v) on entering the inner block. The contents describe a computation which takes place in this four-dimensional state space. After execution of the assignment statement y:= (u + v)/2, the 'auxiliary variables' u and v have done their job and are deleted again by leaving the block: from an operational point of view they cease to exist.

From our syntax it follows that inner blocks can be nested.

Remark. We are free in the choice of **local names** (that is, the names introduced for the local variables in the opening of the inner block). Instead of calling them u and v, we could also have called the local variables p and q, that is, we may just as well have written euclidplus:

```
|[ p, q: int
; p:= y; q:= x
; do x > y  →  x:= x − y; q:= q + p
   ⫿ y > x  →  y:= y − x; p:= p + q
  od
; y:= (p + q)/ 2
]|
```

Texts that can be translated into each other by systematic renaming of local variables are, by definition, equivalent.

For local variables it is sensible not to choose names that already have a meaning in the surroundings of the inner block. (In the wake of Algol 60 many programming languages permit such a double use; our advice is not to.)   ∎

To avoid any misunderstanding, the difference between a functional specification and an inner block, and in particular the different use made of local variables, should be emphasized. A functional specification is an assertion with regard to the initial states, that is, the values of the local variables, which satisfy the given precondition. At the beginning of an inner block the variables introduced in it have no defined values and, as a rule, the first statements of an inner block assign values to the local variables. These values are constants or depend on the state of the surroundings on entering it. The initialization of the local variables typically establishes a relation between local and global variables – the latter are the variables from the surroundings of the inner block – which are then maintained by the statements of the inner block. We have seen this typical use of local variables in euclidplus, and we shall come across it more often.

This is the end of our digression about inner blocks. We return to the repetitive statement.

*   *   *

The description of the postulate of the repetitive statement concluded with 'provided that the repetitive statement terminates', and the promise to return to this extra condition later on. The moment has now come to fulfil this promise.

The following illustrates the fact that this extra condition must indeed be posed:

```
|[ x: int
    {x ≥ 0}
; do x ≠ 0 → x:= x − 1 od
    {x = 0}
]|
```

In the above, the precondition $x \geq 0$ is absolutely essential. Provided that it is satisfied, x denotes exactly how many iterations the repetition terminates after, but for $x < 0$ the repetition will never terminate: after all, it can only terminate with $x = 0$, but after a negative x which can only decrease, it will never become equal to zero.

In a deterministic program the number of iterations after which the repetition terminates is uniquely determined by the initial state. For the sake of completeness it should be mentioned that this does not have to be the case in non-deterministic programs, as is clear from

```
|[ x: int
    {x ≥ 0}
; do x ≠ 0 → x:= x − 1
    ▯ x ≥ 2 → x:= x − 2
    od
    {x = 0}
]|
```

In such a case the initial state determines only an upper bound for the number of iterations that take place.

In both the examples given above $x \geq 0$ is obviously an invariant of the repetitive statement. Moreover, each iteration decreases x by at least 1. The combination of these two facts implies that the possible number of iterations has an upper bound (namely the value of x).

For a repetition with invariant P, an integer function vf of the state must be found, such that the value of vf can be interpreted as the upper bound for the number of iterations.

The postulate of the repetitive statement will once more be formulated, but this time including the termination proof, for the case of two guarded commands (again leaving the generalization more or less to the reader).

Together, the assertions

$$|[\; x, \, y, \, z: \; int \; \{P \; \wedge \; B0 \; \wedge \; vf = VF\}; \; S0 \; \{P \; \wedge \; vf < VF\} \;]|$$
$$|[\; x, \, y, \, z: \; int \; \{P \; \wedge \; B1 \; \wedge \; vf = VF\}; \; S1 \; \{P \; \wedge \; vf < VF\} \;]|$$

and $P \wedge (B0 \vee B1) \Rightarrow vf \geq 0$ in any point of the state space justify the assertion

```
|[ x, y, z: int
   {P}
; do B0 → S0 ▯ B1 → S1 od
   {P ∧ ¬B0 ∧ ¬B1}
]|
```

EXERCISE

Check that for euclid and euclidplus the choice of $vf = x + y$ satisfies the requirements.

Remark. The name of vf is inspired by the historical denotation 'variant function'. We could also have chosen cc, as it is, in fact, a kind of convergence criterion.   ∎

∗   ∗   ∗

EXAMPLE 0

Let Bx be a Boolean expression in the integer x which is not *false* for all natural x. In this case we can try to find the minimal natural x such that Bx holds:

```
|[ x: int {true}
; linear search
   {x is the smallest natural x such that Bx holds}
]|
```

As is often the case, the way to tackle this problem systematically is to formalize the postcondition. It is not sufficient to demand that Bx holds upon completion; we must also express that it is the smallest x, that is, we must also demand that B does not hold for smaller natural numbers. Denoting the analogous Boolean expression in i by Bi, the formal expression for our postcondition is then:

$$(\underline{A}\ i:\ 0 \leq i < x: \neg Bi) \wedge Bx$$

If, as is the case here, the postcondition is a conjunction, a suitable invariant can sometimes be found by leaving out one of the terms of the conjunction of the postcondition: after all, the invariant must be a weakening of the postcondition.

In this case this method would suggest choosing

P: $(\underline{A}\ i:\ 0 \leq i < x: Bi)$

as invariant, particularly since the initialization x:= 0 makes P trivial.

After this choice very little ingenuity is needed for the rest. From the remark that the value 0 could not be too large for x, but may be too small, we can conclude that the program must be able to increase the value of x. The ingenuity then consists of the suggestion of confining ourselves to the assignment statement x:= x + 1.

This leads immediately to the question under which precondition x:= x + 1 leads to a final state in which P is satisfied. Taking into account the definition of P, direct application of the postulate of the assignment statement yields the assertion:

```
|[ x: int { (A i: 0 ≤ i < x + 1: ¬Bi) }
; x:= x + 1 {P}
]|
```

The above precondition, however, can be reduced to:

```
    (A i: 0 ≤ i < x + 1: ¬Bi)
= {definition of universal quantification}
    (A i: 0 ≤ i < x: ¬Bi)  ∧  ¬Bx
= {definition of P}
    P ∧ ¬Bx
```

from which, by substitution, we can derive the assertion

```
|[ x: int {P  ∧  ¬Bx}; x:= x + 1 {P} ]|
```

On condition of termination, the application of the postulate of the repetitive statement yields the following annotated program for linear search:

```
    {true}
    x:= 0 {P}
  ; do ¬Bx  →  x:= x + 1 {P} od
    {P ∧ Bx}
```

On the basis of the definition of P, the above postcondition is exactly the postcondition from the functional specification for linear search. If X is the required answer, the termination can be argued by means of $vf = X - x$. (To this end, the invariant must be strengthened by the additional requirement $0 \le x \le X$.)

Remark. Note that there is no objection whatsoever to involving the eventual answer in the invariant or termination argument.   ∎

The moral of this is that a search in *ascending* order yields a *minimum* value which satisfies some condition; conversely, a search in *decreasing* order yields a *maximum* value. (All this, of course, assumes that the value searched for does indeed exist.) The moral is not deep, but it is so frequently applicable that it deserves a name: it is known as the Linear Search Theorem.

EXAMPLE 1

Consider the functional specification of the program square root, which determines the square root, rounded down, for natural N:

```
|[ N, a: int
   {N = N'  ∧  N ≥ 0}
 ; square root
   {N = N'  ∧  a² ≤ N  ∧  (a + 1)² > N}
]|
```

An abbreviation for functional specifications   This functional specification makes it clear, as appears from its first line, that square root takes place in a state space spanned by two integer variables N and a. However, the term $N = N'$ in the precondition and postcondition expresses the fact that N is not a variable: square root must establish $a^2 \le N \land (a + 1)^2 > N$ on the additional condition that the value of N remains unchanged. (A pseudo-solution, such as $a:= 1; N:= 1$, which does indeed establish $a^2 \le N \land (a + 1)^2 > N$, is therefore rejected.)

To avoid introducing the name N' and dragging along the not very interesting term N = N' all the time, the convention is introduced that, for functional specifications in which the state space is defined with a block and an inner block, the variables introduced in the outer block must be regarded as constants in the inner block. According to this convention the functional specification of **square root** can then be:

```
|[ N: int
 ; |[ a: int
      {N ≥ 0}
    ; square root
      {a² ≤ N ∧ (a + 1)² > N}
   ]|
]|
```

and the term N = N' no longer has to be explicitly stated in all the conditions.   ∎

Since it follows from the postcondition and the monotonicity of the square root that the desired final value of **a** is the smallest natural number for which $(a + 1)^2 > N$, we can immediately apply the Linear Search Theorem and conclude that

a:= 0; <u>do</u> (a + 1)*(a + 1) ≤ N → a:= a + 1 <u>od</u>

satisfies the specification of **square root**.

EXERCISE

Prove directly the correctness of this last solution, that is, without using the Linear Search Theorem. [*Hint*: choose $a^2 ≤ N$ as invariant.]

For large values of N and thus for large eventual values of **a**, the above solution for **square root** is relatively time-consuming, however, because **a** is only incremented by 1 at each iteration. For reasons of efficiency, therefore, it is interesting to look for a solution in which **a** can be incremented in larger steps.

As invariant we choose

P: $a^2 ≤ N$ ∧ $b^2 > N$ ∧ $0 ≤ a < b$

the first two terms of which are obtained by substituting the expression a + 1 by a new variable b in the given postcondition. P then has the interesting property that P ∧   b = a + 1 implies the given postcondition, that our goal can be achieved by a repetitive statement with P as invariant and b ≠ a + 1 as guard. (The latter term puts a further restriction on the range of values: apparently we are not interested in negative values of a, and apparently a is intended to approximate the answer from below and b from above. On introducing new variables, it is always wise to state obvious bounds explicitly.) The following structure is now suggested for square root:

```
|[ b: int {N ≥ 0}
; establish P
; establish b = a + 1 under invariance of P
   {P ∧ b = a + 1 , therefore}
]| {a² ≤ N ∧ (a + 1)² > N}
```

For establish P we may choose

```
a:= 0; b:= 1; do b * b ≤ N → b:= b + 1 od
```

but then establish P could take just as long as our first solution, which we rejected for reasons of efficiency! In short, b must increment much faster, but (see P) we can allow b to outstrip the answer quite a bit. Instead of incrementing by 1, we shall double it:

```
a:= 0; b:= 1; do b * b ≤ N → b:= 2 * b od
```

Not only is b doubled but, because a = 0 still holds, the difference b − a is also doubled; in establish b = a + 1 under invariance of P this difference is just as often halved. This leads to the following solution for square root, more or less fully annotated:

```
|[ b: int {0 ≤ N}
; a:= 0; b:= 1 {a² ≤ N ∨ 0 ≤ a < b}
; do b * b ≤ N → b:= 2 * b {a² ≤ N ∧ 0 ≤ a < b} od {P}
; do b ≠ a + 1 →
        |[ c: int {P ∧ b ≠ a + 1}
        ; c:= (a + b)div 2 {P ∧ a < c < b}
        ; if c * c ≤ N →
                {c² ≤ N ∧ b² > N ∧ 0 ≤ c < b , i.e. Pᵃ_c}
                a:= c {P}
         [] c * c > N →
                {a² ≤ N ∧ c² > N ∧ 0 ≤ a < c , i.e. Pᵇ_c}
                b:= c {P}
          fi {P}
        ]| {P}
      od {P ∧ b = a + 1, therefore}
]| {a² ≤ N ∧ (a + 1)² > N}
```

EXERCISES

- Verify the foregoing annotation.
- Find a termination argument for the first repetitive statement.
- Find a termination argument for the second repetitive statement which would also be valid if the guards of the alternative statement were both replaced by true.
- Show that P can be strengthened to:

  $$P \wedge (\underline{E} \; i: \; i \geq 0: \; (b - a) = 2^i)$$

- Show that therefore c:= (a + b)$\underline{div}$ 2 can be replaced by c:= (a + b)/ 2.

Whereas in our first program – the Linear Search – the required number of iterations equalled $\sqrt{N}$, in our new program this number is proportional to log N.

Remark. The new program is a modification of the algorithm to determine whether a given value occurs in a sorted list, which is known by the name of Binary Search, and will be dealt with later.   ■

EXAMPLE 2

Consider the functional specification:

```
|[ X, Y: int
 ; |[ z: int {Y ≥ 0}
    ; exponentiation {z = Xʸ, compare Remark}
    ]|
 ]|
```

Remark. We agree that $X^0 = 1$ for all values of X, therefore also for X = 0.   ■

According to its functional specification it is the job of exponentiation to raise a given number X to a natural power Y. Our solutions are based on a repetitive statement with an invariant P of the form

P: $z \cdot h = X^Y$

which has the pleasant property that we may conclude from

$$P \land h = 1$$

that the postcondition holds.

Remark. If we had written the postcondition as

$$z \cdot 1 = X^Y$$

then again the invariant would have been obtained by substituting a subexpression in the postcondition, in this case the constant 1, by a variable. The substitution of an 'invisible' constant is not uncommon. ∎

The initial validity of P could be established by the assignment statements

$$z := 1; \ h := X^Y$$

if it were not for the fact that in this form the initialization of the auxiliary variable would require the solution of the original problem. Since h is only an auxiliary variable, we can represent its value in another way, and we choose a representation for h which overcomes this initialization problem.

$$h = X^y$$

According to this convention the value of h is represented by means of a local variable y. After substitution we have for the invariant (supplemented with bounds for y)

$$P: \quad z \cdot X^y = X^Y \ \land \ y \geq 0$$

the initial validity of P can be established by $z := 1; \ y := Y$, and since $y = 0 \Rightarrow h = 1$, it is sufficient when the next repetitive statement establishes $y = 0$ under invariance of P. All this leads to the following solution for exponentiation:

```
|[ y: int {Y ≥ 0}
; z:= 1; y:= Y {P}
; do y ≠ 0  →  z:= z * X; y:= y − 1 {P} od
  {P ∧ y = 0, therefore}
]| {z = X^Y}
```

EXERCISE

Verify the annotation in this program, and formulate the termination argument.

The program requires a number of iterations equal to Y, the initial value of y, which is decremented by 1 at each iteration until we have y = 0. But we know of more effective ways to reduce a variable, such as halving. To this end a second variable is introduced for the representation of h.

$$h = x^y$$

According to this convention the value of h is represented by means of the local variables x and y. After substitution we have for the invariant (again supplemented with bounds for y)

$$P: \quad z \cdot x^y = X^Y \wedge y \geq 0$$

the original validity of P can now be established by z:= 1; x:= X; y:= Y; again the problem is to reach y = 0 under invariance of P. For even y, i.e. y mod 2 = 0, halving y is generally a more drastic way of decrementing than y:= y − 1; the invariance of P is guaranteed when halving y is accompanied by raising x to its square.

By adding the guarded command

$$y \neq 0 \ \wedge \ y \bmod 2 = 0 \ \rightarrow \ x:= x * x; \ y:= y \ / \ 2$$

which does not interfere with P, we initially get the following for exponentiation:

```
|[ x, y: int {Y ≥ 0}
; z:= 1; x:= X; y:= Y {P}
; do y ≠ 0  →  z:= x * z; y:= y − 1 {P}
   [] y ≠ 0  ∧  y mod 2 = 0  →  x:= x * x; y:= y / 2 {P}
   od {P ∧ y = 0, therefore}
]| {z = Xʸ}
```

For larger values of Y this program could work more efficiently, namely, when the second guarded command is selected for execution, if this is possible. In the above non-deterministic program this gain, however, is not always guaranteed, because it is always possible that the first guarded command would be chosen. However, we can ensure the gain by strengthening the first guard, and by conjugating it with the negation of the second one, so that the first possibility is chosen only when the second one does not apply. Since (check this!):

$$(y \neq 0 \;\wedge\; \neg(y \neq 0 \;\wedge\; y \bmod 2 = 0)) \equiv$$
$$(y \bmod 2 \neq 0)$$

this removal of non-determinism leads (this time without annotation) to:

```
|[ x, y: int; z:= 1; x:= X; y:= Y
 ; do y mod 2 ≠ 0  →  z:= x * z; y:= y − 1
    ▯ y ≠ 0  ∧  y mod 2 = 0  →  x:= x * x; y:= y / 2
   od
 ]|
```

There are many ways in which one can try to 'accelerate' the above algorithm for exponentiation. For example, the computation of the product $x * z$ is not necessary the first time because $z = 1$, therefore the product is x. Or, for example, one could try to exploit the fact that immediately after $y:= y − 1$, $y \bmod 2 = 0$ apparently holds. All such attempts probably make the program text less clear, and in any case much longer. Moreover, such marginal improvements are, of course, only crumbs compared to what was gained by changing from a linear to a logarithmic algorithm.

There was a time when constructing the fastest program, irrespective of cost, was considered profoundest wisdom. Now, fortunately, this has become obsolete: we know that the Law of Diminishing Returns would have to be paid for in the end, that the price of complexity cannot be overestimated, that compact elegance is of far greater importance, and that we do much better by leaving the crumbs for what they are. The selection of the right algorithm is far more effective. By the elegance of their programs professionals are distinguished from amateurs.

The array

Something quite essential is still missing from our program notation. The introduction of the repetitive statement was motivated by the consideration that it should be possible for a short program text to initiate an arbitrarily long-lasting computation process. A similar kind of consideration demands that it should be possible for a short program text to process an arbitrary quantity of data. This means that it should be possible for the same program text to refer to a state space of an arbitrary, but for practical reasons finite, number of dimensions. As long as we have to list the individual coordinates of the state space one by one, as we did up to now, we can never meet this demand. Therefore we shall give our program notation the minimal extension that will enable us to introduce an arbitrary number of integers or Booleans in a single declaration. We shall first illustrate this by an example.

For example, the opening of the functional specification

```
|[ N: int {N ≥ 1}
; f(i: 0 ≤ i < N): array of int
; |[
```

implies that the rest, which is left out, must be understood in a constant environment consisting of the positive integer N and a sequence of N integers, called $f(0)$, $f(1)$, . . . , $f(N-1)$, respectively.

Remark. In the above explanation the name i, which occurs in the declaration of f, is no longer present. That is because this i in the program text is only a dummy: the second line could just as well have been

```
; f(x: 0 ≤ x < N): array of int
```

Since we shall confine ourselves to dummies of type *integer*, we shall *not* explicitly state the type of the dummies in declarations of arrays.

∎

The integers $f(0), f(1), \ldots, f(N-1)$ are called 'the elements of the array f' and i is called the 'index' or 'subscript' of element $f(i)$, for $0 \le i < N$. The syntax for array elements in our program text is:

$$\langle array\ element \rangle ::= \langle name \rangle\ (\ \langle integer\ expression \rangle\ )$$

that is, the name of the array followed by an integer expression in brackets as a definition of the intended index value.

To show how we can work with arrays and their elements, the complete opening of the above functional specification is given:

```
|[ N: int {N ≥ 1}
; f(i: 0 ≤ i < N): array of int
; |[ s: int
    ; summation
      {s = (S i: 0 ≤ i < N: f(i))}
    ]|
]|
```

that is, in the final state the value of s must equal the sum of the elements of f. For our invariant P we choose:

$$P: \quad s = (\underline{S}\ i: 0 \le i < n: f(i)) \ \wedge\ 0 \le n \le N$$

obtained, not unexpectedly, by replacing the constant N in the postcondition by a new variable, say n, and by limiting its range of values, just as expected. All this yields the following solution for summation:

```
|[ n: int
; s:= 0; n:= 0
; do n ≠ N  →  s:= s + f(n); n:= n + 1 od
]|
```

Remark. A functional specification becomes more demanding, or 'stronger', if we weaken the precondition. In this way we can strengthen the functional specification of summation by weakening the precondition to $N \ge 0$. Check that the above solution also satisfies this stronger specification. Which solution satisfies the original specification of summation but not the strengthened one? ■

In the solution for summation we have craftily used an extension of the syntax of integer expressions not given before. To this end we extend the syntax for an *intfactor* to:

⟨ *intfactor* ⟩
     ::= ⟨ *natural number* ⟩
       | ⟨ *name* ⟩
       | ⟨ *array element* ⟩
       | (⟨ *integer expression* ⟩)

In the above example we introduced a sequence of integers by `array of` int. Quite analogously we can introduce a sequence of Booleans by `array of` bool. The corresponding extension of the syntax for Boolean expressions is done by permitting a new form for the Boolean primary:

Boolean primary
     ::= *true*
       | *false*
       | ⟨ *name* ⟩
       | ⟨ *array element* ⟩
       | ⟨ *integer expression* ⟩ ⟨ *relop* ⟩ ⟨ *integer expression* ⟩
       | (⟨ *Boolean expression* ⟩)

As another example, consider the functional specification of `maxlocation`:

```
|[ N: int; f(i: 0 ≤ i < N): array of int {N ≥ 1}
; |[ k: int
   ; maxlocation
      {0 ≤ k < N ∧  (A i: 0 ≤ i < N: f(i) ≤ f(k))}
   ]|
]|
```

Note that the postcondition, regarded as an equation in k, can always be solved because $N \geq 1$, but that this solution is not necessarily unique. So we can expect to find a non-deterministic program for `maxlocation`.

EXERCISE

Give a sufficient condition for the final value of k to be determined uniquely.

As in the last example, we choose for our invariant P after introduction of a new variable n

P: $0 \leq k < n$ ∧ (A i: $0 \leq i < n$: $f(i) \leq f(k)$ ∧ $1 \leq n \leq N$

which on the basis of its construction again justifies the conclusion that
the postcondition is satisfied if $P \wedge n = N$.

Since (check this!)

$$P \wedge n \neq N \wedge f(n) \leq f(k) \Rightarrow P^n_{n+1}$$

the postulate of the assignment statement justifies the assertion

```
|[ N, k, n: int; f(i: 0 ≤ i < N): array of int
   {P ∧ n ≠ N ∧ f(n) ≤ f(k)}
 ; n:= n + 1
   {P}
 ]|
```

The above assertion tells us under which additional condition
increasing $n := n + 1$ does not interfere with the validity of P. By a possible
modification of k we can see to it that this additional condition is also
satisfied since, owing to the postulate of the assignment statement and the
transitivity of the relation $\leq$, we have:

```
|[ N, k, n: int; f(i: 0 ≤ i < N): array of int
   {P ∧ n ≠ N ∧ f(n) ≥ f(k)}
 ; k:= n
   {P^n_{n+1}}
 ]|
```

EXERCISE

Prove this assertion.

A combination of the above observations yields the following
solution for maxlocation:

```
|[ n: int
 ; k:= 0; n:= 1
 ; do n ≠ N  →  if f(n) ≤ f(k)  →  skip
                 ◻ f(n) ≥ f(k)  →  k:= n
                fi; n:= n + 1
   od
 ]|
```

EXERCISE

Give the necessary annotation for this solution and complete the correctness proof.

$$*\qquad *\qquad *$$

In both these examples the array f was constant, and all the program had to do was to determine the suitable value of a variable of the type *integer* – in the first example the value of s, in the second the value of k. Now we shall look at an example in which the program must compute the value of the array, that is, modify it if necessary, so that the postcondition is satisfied. This is the program upsort, whose functional specification is as follows:

```
|[ N: int {N ≥ 1}
 ; |[ f(i: 0 ≤ i < N): array of int
      {(B i: 0 ≤ i < N: f(i)) = X}
    ; upsort
      {(B i: 0 ≤ i < N: f(i)) = X ∧
       (A i, j: 0 ≤ i < j  ∧  1 ≤ j < N: f(i) ≤ f(j))}
    ]|
 ]|
```

Let us first analyse this functional specification carefully. For a given array $f(i: 0 \le i < N)$, $(B\ i: 0 \le i < N: f(i))$ denotes the bag obtained by collecting N numbers from the sequence $f(i: 0 \le i < N)$ in a bag; therefore the constant X from the precondition and postcondition stands for a bag holding N integers. So the precondition and the first line of the postcondition express the fact that collecting the numbers from the sequence $f(i: 0 \le i < N)$ yields the same bag before and after execution of upsort, in other words that so far as the sequence of numbers $f(i: 0 \le i < N)$ is concerned the execution of upsort effects only a permutation, i.e. a change of the order, of these numbers. The second line specifies formally what the final order must satisfy: eventually, the numbers in the sequence $f(i: 0 \le i < N)$ must be in ascending order. (Equal numbers within the sequence not being excluded, f is called 'ascending' upon completion; only if they are all different from one another is the result called 'increasing'.)

We obtain the invariant P of our solution for upsort by substituting by a new variable, let us say q, for the constant 1 in the postcondition:

P: $(\underline{B}\ i: 0 \le i < N: f(i)) = X \ \wedge\ 1 \le q \le N \ \wedge$
      $(\underline{A}\ i, j: 0 \le i < j \ \wedge\ q \le j < N: f(i) \le f(j))$

so that we may conclude from P $\wedge$ q = 1 that the postcondition is satisfied.

Remark. Our choice of P seems quite arbitrary, and so it is. Many other choices for P are possible; they lead us to as many other solutions for upsort: the development of sorting routines is a well trodden path.   ■

Before we go on, it is worth analysing carefully exactly what the second line of P implies. Because $q \le j < N$, $f(j)$ denotes one of the last $N - q$ numbers of the sequence $f(i: 0 \le i < N)$; because $0 \le i < j$, P implies that none of these last $N - q$ numbers is anywhere preceded by a larger one. In other words, the subsequence $f(j: q \le j < N)$ has its final value, so that the rest of the computation can be confined to a possible permutation of $f(i: 0 \le i < q)$.

The obvious structure of upsort is now:

```
|[ q: int {N ≥ 1}; q:= N {P}
; do q ≠ 1 →  'q:= q − 1 under invariance of P' od
]|
```

Because of the postulate of the assignment this structure evokes interest in P_{q-1}^q. Now $R \Rightarrow p_{q-1}^q$ holds with:

R: $P \ \wedge\ q \ne 1 \ \wedge\ (\underline{A}\ i: 0 \le i < q: f(i) \le f(q - 1))$

EXERCISE

Check this assertion carefully.

We do not have to worry much about the first two terms of R: the first is the invariant and the second is the guard. It is the last term that requires our attention: it implies that $f(q - 1)$, i.e. the last number of the subsequence $f(i: 0 \le i < q)$, is not preceded by a larger number.

This is the moment to recall the functional specification of maxlocation: the postcondition of maxlocation indicates that k has a value such that $f(k)$ is a maximal value of the sequence. The only difference is that instead of being interested in the sequence $f(i: 0 \le i < N)$, for which maxlocation is formulated, we are now interested in the position of the maximum of the sequence $f(i: 0 \leq i < q)$; we modify maxlocation for our purposes by changing to a version in which N is replaced by q. Using a version of maxlocation thus modified enables us to establish

$$(\underline{A} \ i: 0 \leq i < q: f(i) \leq f(k))$$

but our objective is to establish the last term of R

$$(\underline{A} \ i: 0 \leq i < q: f(i) \leq f(q - 1)$$

by exchanging elements of the sequence $f(i: 0 \leq i < q)$: the 'new' $f(q - 1)$ must become equal to the 'old' $f(k)$. In the sequence $f(i: 0 \leq i < q)$ the values with indexes k and $q - 1$, respectively, must change places.

Exchanging two elements of an array is so frequent an operation that a special statement is used called the swap. Execution of

    f:swap(k, q − 1)

realizes the change desired in our case; if $k = q - 1$, i.e. the exchange of an element with itself, the execution of swap given above is then equivalent to a skip. Before going into this operation, we shall first complete our discussion of upsort:

```
|[ q: int {N ≥ 1}; q:= N {P}
; do q ≠ 1 →
      |[ k: int
      ; |[ n: int; k:= 0; n:= 1
         ; do n ≠ q  →  if  f(n) ≤ f(k)  →  skip
                          ▯ f(n) ≥ f(k)  →  k  := n
                        fi; n:= n + 1
           od
        ]|
      ; f:swap(k, q − 1) {R}
      ]| ; q:= q − 1
  od
]|
```

                    *   *   *

We need a new notation for the formal definition of the semantics of swap, which is an example of an **array modifier**.

The value of a variable of the type array of ... is a function defined on a finite number of integers which together form the **domain** of the function. f and g are the same function is expressed by

$$(\underline{A} \; i :: f(i) = g(i))$$

in which $f(i) = g(i)$ is considered to hold when i is outside the domain of either – something like undefined = undefined – but not when i is within the one domain but not in the other – something like defined $\neq$ undefined; with this convention we have captured the fact that, to be equal, functions must at least have the same domain.

We are now interested in a function g, which differs only very slightly from f, perhaps at only one point h, for example; more precisely, we consider the relation:

$$g(h) = p \; \wedge \; (\underline{A}i: i \neq h: f(i) = g(i))$$

The function g which satisfies this relation is written as (f; h: p). If h belongs to the domain of f, (f; h: p) has the same domain, otherwise the domain of (f; h: p) is the domain of f, extended with the point h.

From the definition there follows the calculation rules:

$$(f; h: p) \; (i) = p \qquad \text{if} \quad i = h$$
$$(f; h: p) \; (i) = f(i) \qquad \text{if} \quad i \neq h$$

Remark. The reader who is frightened by the idea of an expression like (f; h: p) representing a function should realize that the idea is quite familiar from differential calculus.   ■

Use of (f; h: p) is postponed for the moment; in connection with swap, our greatest interest is rather a function of g which can differ from the domain of f in two points, i.e. which (for some h, k, p and q) satisfies

$$g(h) = p \; \wedge \; g(k) = q \; \wedge \; (\underline{A} \; i: i \neq h \; \wedge \; i \neq k: f(i) = g(i))$$

Remark. There is no such g for $h = k \; \wedge \; p \neq q$; but for $h \neq k \; \vee \; p = q$ there is always such a g.   ■

On the assumption of $h \neq k \; \vee \; p = q$, the function g which satisfies the above relation is written as (f; h, k: p, q). From this definition there follows the calculation rules:

```
(f; h, k: p, q) (i) = p      if  i = h
(f; h, k: p, q) (i) = q      if  i = k
(f; h, k: p, q) (i) = f(i)   if  i ≠ h  ∧  i ≠ k
```

And now we have the – albeit laborious – tool to define the semantics of swap. For a variable f of the type <u>array of</u> ... the semantics of f:swap(h, k) is the same as that of the assignment statement

```
f:= (f; h, k: f(k), f(h))
```

(which, by the way, is not permitted in programs).
Application of the postulate of assignment yields the structure of the general assertion about swap:

```
|[ h, k: int; f(......): array of ...
   {R^f_(f; h, k: f(k), f(h))}
 ; f:swap(h, k)
   {R}
]|
```

EXERCISES

- Demonstrate the correctness of:

```
|[ h, k: int; f(......): array of ...
   {R  ∧  f(h) = f(k)}
 ; f:swap(h, k)
   {R  ∧  f(h) = f(k)}
]|
```

for arbitrary R.
     In other words, with the additional condition f(h) = f(k), f:swap(h, k) operates like a skip; a consequence of this theorem is that this is also the case for the additional condition h = k.

- Demonstrate the correctness of

```
|[ h, k: int; f(......): array of ...
   {R}
 ; f:swap(h, k); f:swap(h, k)
   {R}
]|
```

for arbitrary R.
     In other words the operation f:swap(h, k) is its own inverse.

Remark. Where a and b are variables of the same type <u>array of</u> ... , there would not be any logical objection to permitting an assignment statement of the form a:= b for arrays in our programs; for reasons of uniformity it is even attractive. For two practical reasons, however, we shall *not* introduce the general assignment to the array variable.

The first practical reason is that, in almost all implementation techniques, the execution of an array assignment a:= b generally takes far more time than the integer assignment x:= y. Always keeping the efficiency of our programs in the back of our minds, we regard x:= y as a primitive, but not the time-consuming a:= b. In this respect it would be misleading to write both operations in exactly the same way.

The second practical reason is that it would be very inviting to introduce permissible expressions of the type <u>array of</u> ... , just as we did for integers and Booleans. But whereas the number of meaningful operators is so limited for simple types, such as integer and Boolean, that you introduce them 'all', so to speak, for arrays there is a vast crowd of them. Not only does this make it very difficult to make a defensible selection – Iverson tried to do this in the design of APL – but even worse, one should also develop – and master! – the rules according to which such expressions can be manipulated and, what is more, simplified (particularly in proofs). (This is why it is unusual for the correctness of APL programs to be demonstrated.)   ∎

The formalism (f; h, k: f(k), f(h)) for the denotation of the array formed by the modifier f:swap(h, k) is too laborious to be used frequently. We gave it to underline the fact that these modifiers should be regarded as operators on the 'whole' array, and for the sake of completeness. In actual practice this formalism is hardly ever used directly; it is used instead on theorems that can be proved by means of the formalism. A few examples are:

(i)   The statements f:swap(h, k) and f:swap(k, h) are semantically equivalent.

(ii) |[h, k, z, N: int; f(i: 0 ≤ i < N): <u>array of</u> int
       {h = H ∧ k = K ∧ z = Z ∧ N = M ∧ 0 ≤ h, k < N}
       ; f:swap(h, k)
       {h = H ∧ k = K ∧ z = Z ∧ N = M ∧ 0 ≤ h, k < N}
       ]|

(iii) |[h, k, N: int; f(i: 0 ≤ i < N): <u>array of</u> int
       {f(h) = X ∧ f(k) = Y}
       ; f:swap(h, k)
       {f(k) = X ∧ f(h) = Y}
       ]|

(iv) |[h, k, z, N: int; f(i: 0 ≤ i < N): <u>array of</u> int
        {z ≠ h ∧ z ≠ k ∧ f(z) = X}
        ; f:swap(h, k)
        {z ≠ h ∧ z ≠ k ∧ f(z) = X}
        ]|

(v) |[h, k, N: int; f(i: 0 ≤ i < N): <u>array of</u> int
        {0 ≤ A ≤ B ≤ N ∧ A ≤ h < B ∧ A ≤ k < B ∧
            (<u>B</u> i: A ≤ i < B: f(i)) = X}
        ; f:swap(h, k)
        {(<u>B</u> i: A ≤ i < B: f(i)) = X}
        ]|

As another example of the use of **swap** we develop a program that satisfies the following functional specification for **rotation**:

    |[k, N: int {N ≥ 1 ∧ 0 ≤ k < N}
    ; |[f(i: 0 ≤ i < N): <u>array of</u> int
        {(<u>A</u> i: 0 ≤ i < N: f(i) = X((k + i)<u>mod</u> N))}
        ; rotation
        {(<u>A</u> i: 0 ≤ i < N: f(i) = X(i))}
        ]|
    ]|

Again we start with a careful analysis of what this functional specification implies. Apparently, we may identify the sequence X(i: 0 ≤ i < N) with the final value of array f. It follows from the precondition that originally all elements of sequence X also occur in array f, but in a different position.

By way of analysing the precondition, let us first eliminate the operation <u>mod</u> N from it by separating the cases i + k < N from the cases i + k ≥ N. The precondition then becomes:

    (<u>A</u> i: 0 ≤ i < N − k: f(i) = X(k + i)) ∧
    (<u>A</u> i: N − k ≤ i < N: f(i) = X(k + i − N))

We can write this a little more symmetrically using a constant h given by:

    h + k = N

and by replacing i in the second term by h + j. We then get:

    (<u>A</u> i: 0 ≤ i < h: f(i) = X(k + i)) ∧
    (<u>A</u> j: 0 ≤ j < k: f(h + j) = X(j))

As an abbreviation we shall call the subsequence X(j: 0 ≤ j < k),

K, and the subsequence $X(i: k \leq i < k + h)$, H. Denoting concatenation of sequences by ·, we then have

$X = K \cdot H$

and the postcondition is thus

$f = K \cdot H$

and the precondition

$f = H \cdot K$

In short: the subsequences H and K must 'change places', but we have put it in inverted commas, because the two subsequences need not be equally long.

For an arbitrary sequence R of finite length, rev R (from 'reverse') denotes the sequence with the same elements as R, but in reverse order, that is,

$rev(rev R) = R$ for any R

More important for our purposes is the proposition

$rev(H \cdot K) = (rev K) \cdot (rev H)$

which leads to the following solution for rotation:

```
|[ x, y: int
   {f = H · K}
 ; x:= 0; y:= N - 1
 ; do x < y → f:swap(x, y); x:= x + 1; y:= y - 1 od
   {f = (rev K) · (rev H)}
 ; x:= k; y:= N - 1
 ; do x < y → f:swap(x, y); x:= x + 1; y:= y - 1 od
   {f = (rev K) · H}
 ; x:= 0; y:= k - 1
 ; do x < y → f:swap(x, y); x:= x + 1; y:= y - 1 od
   {f = K · H}
]|
```

EXERCISE

Prove the correctness of the subprogram, for example for the first application of rev. Contrary to the program text, a distinction will probably have to be made between N even and N odd in the proof.

Remark. In most program notations some kind of abbreviation mechanism is available, so that one is not obliged to give such repetitions of the text.   ■

There is a quite different solution for rotation, based on the following consideration. From the initial state

$$f = H \cdot K$$

the final state

$$f = K \cdot H$$

must be achieved. Now we consider the case where H is at least as long as K. In this case we can write H as H0 · H1, where H0 is as long as K. If we substitute this, the transition from

$$f = H0 \cdot H1 \cdot K \quad \text{to} \quad f = K \cdot H0 \cdot H1$$

must then be realized. Since H0 and K are equally long, the transition from

$$f = H0 \cdot H1 \cdot K \quad \text{to} \quad f = K \cdot H1 \cdot H0$$

can be easily realized by exchanging the subsequences H0 and K. Then there still remains the transition from

$$f = K \cdot H1 \cdot H0 \quad \text{to} \quad f = K \cdot H0 \cdot H1$$

which is an operation of the same kind as the original, but this time on the shorter subsequence H1 · H0. The case that K is at least equally long as H can be dealt with in a similar way, namely, by splitting up K as a concatenation of two subsequences, of which the latter part is as long as H. In this way we get an algorithm in which at each step either the number of elements at the head of f or the number of elements at the tail of f, which have their definitive values, is extended.

We introduce four variables, p and q so that the first p elements of f and the last $N - q$ elements of f have their definitive values, and r and s which describe how the intermediate values of f must still be rotated. The global invariant of our program becomes:

$$P: \quad 0 \leq p \leq N \ \wedge \ 0 \leq q \leq N \ \wedge \ 0 \leq r \ \wedge \ 0 \leq s \ \wedge \ p + s + r = q \ \wedge$$
$$(\underline{A} \ i: 0 \leq i < p \ \vee \ q \leq i < N: f(i) = X(i)) \ \wedge$$
$$(\underline{A} \ i: p \leq i < p + r: f(i) = X(i + s)) \ \wedge$$
$$(\underline{A} \ i: q - s \leq i < q: f(i) = X(i - r))$$

On the basis of the precondition the initialization

$$p:= 0; \ q:= N; \ s:= k; \ r:= N - k$$

establishes the invariant P. Furthermore, the postcondition follows from
$P \land (r = 0 \lor s = 0)$.

We shall now demonstrate:

(1)   how, in the case $0 < s \le r$, p can be incremented by s, and r
       decremented by s, under invariance of P;

(2)   how in the case $0 < r \le s$, q and s can both be decremented by r
       under invariance of P.

$0 < s \le r$

The assignments $p:= p + s; \ r:= r - s$ leave the first line of P undisturbed.
The precondition that upon completion the remaining lines of P hold for
this pair is (thanks to the postulate of the assignment):

$$(A \ i: 0 \le i < p + s \ \lor \ q \le i < N: f(i) = X(i)) \ \land$$
$$(A \ i: p + s \le i < p + r: f(i) = X(i + s)) \ \land$$
$$(A \ i: q - s \le i < q: f(i) = X(i - r + s))$$

If we substitute i in the last line by $i + r$, we obtain (after some
simplification):

$$(A \ i: p \le i < p + s: f(i + r) = X(i + s))$$

and by splitting the terms in s from the first line, $p + s < q$, we get for our
precondition:

$$(A \ i: 0 \le i < p \ \lor \ q \le i < N: f(i) = X(i)) \ \land$$
$$(A \ i: p + s \le i < p + r: f(i) = X(i + s)) \ \land$$
$$(A \ i: p \le i < p + s: f(i) = X(i) \ \land \ f(i + r) = X(i + s))$$

By also substituting $i + r$ for i in the last line of P, we get for the
last three lines of P $(0 < s \le r)$

$$(A \ i: 0 \le i < p \ \lor \ q \le i < N: f(i) = X(i)) \ \land$$
$$(A \ i: p + s \le i < p + r: f(i) = X(i + s)) \ \land$$
$$(A \ i: p \le i < p + s: f(i) = X(i + s) \ \land \ f(i + r) = X(i))$$

and after these derivations we see that our precondition for $p:= p + s;$
$r:= r - s$ differs from P only in the last line: from P we can establish the
precondition by executing $f:\text{swap}(i, i + r)$ for $i: p \le i < p + s$.

$$0 < r \leqq s$$

We leave the analysis of this case to the reader as an exercise.

After the requested supplement these reflections lead to the following solution for rotation:

```
|[ p, q, r, s: int
; p:= 0; q:= N; s := k; r:= N − k
; do r ≠ 0 ∧ s ≠ 0 →
      |[ i: int
      ; if s ≦ r →
             i:= p
           ; do i ≠ p + s → f:swap(i, i + r); i:= i + 1 od
           ; p:= p + s; r:= r − s
        []  r ≦ s →
             i:= q − r
           ; do i ≠ q → f:swap(i, i − s); i:= i + 1 od
           ; q:= q − r; s:= s− r
        fi
      ]|
   od
]|
```

Remark. If we concentrate our attention on r and s in this solution, we recognize Euclid's algorithm for the greatest common divisor. Readers are invited to satisfy themselves that the total number of times that f:swap is executed in this version of rotation equals $n − gcd(N, k)$.   ∎

The attentive reader will certainly have noticed that we have developed the two solutions for rotation in rather different styles.

In the first development the sequence f was interpreted as a concatenation of two subsequences and the precondition, intermediate condition, and postcondition were therefore formulated by giving a formula for the sequence for the sequence f (by means of the function rev). The individual elements of array f were no longer mentioned.

In the second development we set out in the same way, but eventually formulated the invariant and made the detailed analysis in terms of the individual elements of the array f. The second development shows that formal analysis is possible and that it neatly yields which swaps must be executed. There is a drawback, however: it is possible to lose sight of the wood for the trees.

The first development does not have this drawback so much. There the array and its individual elements are hardly mentioned: an array representing a sequence is defined once, and then the argument is in terms of sequences. This more indirect method contributes to the brevity of the argument, and is therefore to be preferred. However, in this example, the definition of how an array represents a sequence was quite trivial. As soon as arrays are used to represent more complicated structures – trees, graphs in general, point sets, etc. – the indirect method requires that the definition for the representation is formulated precisely and completely.

Finally, a second and last array modifier will be introduced. After all, swap alone is not sufficient: it permutes values already present in the array but does not enable us to change or extend the collection of values present in the array. We definitely need such a facility, since the declaration of a local array in an inner block introduces an array which does not yet have any values.

Recall the meaning of the notation (f; h: p). Let f be an array (i.e. either array of int or array of bool), let h be an integer expression, and p an (integer or Boolean) expression. Then (f; h: p) is a new array value given by:

$$(f; h: p) (i) = p \quad \text{if} \quad i = h$$
$$(f; h: p) (i) = f(i) \text{ if } \quad i \neq h$$

In other words, (f; h: p) differs only very little from f: regarded as functions on the natural numbers, they correspond everywhere, with the possible exception of point h; here (f; h: p) has the value of p in any case, independently of f, which could even be undefined in that point.

Our last array modifier has the semantics of the assignment statement which, by the way, is not permitted in our programs

$$f := (f; h: p)$$

and is written in our programs as

$$f: (h) = p$$

Application of the postulate of the assignment yields the structure of the general assertion about this array modifier:

```
|[ f(......) : array of
    {R^f_{(f; E0 : E1)}}
  ; f: (E0) = E1
    {R}
]|
```

where E0 is an integer expression and E1 an expression of the same type as the elements of f.

Remark. To those who want to pronounce f: (E0) = E1 we offer the suggestion 'f becomes, in E0, equal to E1'.   ∎

Remark. The introduction of this 'elementary modifier' makes the swap introduced earlier redundant, if only for purely logical reasons. For an integer array f

        f:swap(h, k)

has the same effect as the inner block

        |[x: int
        ; x:= f(h); f:(h) = f(k); f:(k) = x
        ]|

an equivalence of which the reader can be satisfied with in various ways. We shall not draw the logical conclusion from this equivalence to remove swap again.   ∎

As an example, the following program is presented which, given the decimal digits of two (non-negative) numbers, computes the decimal digits of the sum. The functional specification of deciplus is

        |[N: int {N ≥ 0}
        ; a, b(i: 0 ≤ i < N): <u>array of</u> int
          {(<u>A</u> i: 0 ≤ i < N: 0 ≤ a(i) < 10 ∧ 0 ≤ b(i) < 10)}
        ; |[s(i: 0 ≤ i < N + 1): <u>array of</u> int
          ; deciplus
            {(<u>A</u> i: 0 ≤ i < N + 1: 0 ≤ s(i) < 10) ∧
            dec(N + 1, s) = dec(N, a) + dec(N, b)}
          ]|
        ]|

in which the function dec is used. This adds to a sequence of digits the value corresponding to the decimal representation of that sequence of digits. More precisely:

        dec(n, x) = (<u>S</u> i: 0 ≤ i < n: x(i) · 10^i)

Note that array s has one element more than arrays a and b in the functional specification.

It is left to the reader to design the invariant and to give the correctness proof of the program that follows. Variable c (for 'carry') plays the part of 'carry 1', which we all know from school. (Include the bounds for c in the invariant, so that it can be proved that the elements of s satisfy the given inequalities.)

The following is one solution for deciplus:

```
|[ n, c: int
; n:= 0; c:= 0
; do n ≠ N →
      |[ z: int
      ; z:= c + a(n) + b(n)
      ; if  z ≥ 10  →  s:(n) = z - 10; c:= 1
         ▯ z < 10  →  s:(n) = z; c:= 0
         fi ; n:= n + 1
      ]|
  od
; s:(n) = c
]|
```

The last line of the postcondition uses the function dec. This simplifies not only the formulation of the postcondition but also that of the invariant and the correctness proof, which uses the following proposition about dec:

$$dec(n + 1, x) = dec(n, x) + x(n) \cdot 10^n$$

(This is rather impressively called a proposition but it hardly deserves the name, as it follows directly from the recursive definition of the summation S.)

In passing it should be noted that the individual array elements have retreated a little into the background: the argument is conducted largely in terms of the function dec, defined by (a large part of) arrays.

EXERCISE

With $a(i: 0 \leq i < M)$, $b(i: 0 \leq i < N)$ and $s(i: 0 \leq i < M + N)$ we can pose the analogous problem, decitimes, of digit-wise decimal multiplication. Formulate the functional specification whose second line must be

; $a(i: 0 \leq i < M)$, $b(i: 0 \leq i < N)$: <u>array of</u> int

and solve the problem thus posed without introducing local arrays, on the additional condition that even during execution none of the elements of s becomes larger than 9.

This completes the introduction to the program notation, albeit leaving the last extension of the formal syntax for arrays to the reader by way of exercise. The rest of this book is devoted to a collection of examples, in which various solution strategies will be demonstrated.

The minimal segment sum

For an integer array f(i: 0 ≤ i < N), the segment sum Q(i, j) for 0 ≤ i ≤ j ≤ N is defined by:

Q(i, j) = (S h: i ≤ h < j: f(h))

(Note that sums of empty segments are also permitted and that if f is empty, i.e. N = 0, the (empty) segment sum Q(0, 0) is still defined.) The aim is to determine the minimal segment sum; more precisely, to find a solution for minsegsum, specified by:

```
|[ N: int {N ≥ 0}
 ; f(i: 0 ≤ i < N): array of int
 ; |[ x: int
    ; minsegsum
       {x = (MIN i, j: 0 ≤ i ≤ j ≤ N: Q(i, j))}
    ]|
 ]|
```

The number of pairs (i, j), over which the minimum Q(i, j) must be determined, is (N + 1) · (N + 2)/ 2; for a given pair (i, j) the computation of Q(i, j) requires a computation time proportional to j − i, and the most naïve program would therefore require a computation time proportional to N^3. However, it can be done rather more efficiently! (Since each element of array f must be involved in the computation process at least once, it should be obvious that a computation time proportional to N is the best we can hope for.)

With a view to the postcondition, we choose, as usual, to begin with P0 for the invariant, given by:

P0:   0 ≤ n ≤ N ∧ x = (MIN i, j: 0 ≤ i ≤ j ≤ n: Q(i, j))

This invariant is particularly attractive because, according to the definition of $Q(i, j)$, the elements of $f(i: n \leq i < N)$ do not occur in P0. For an algorithm with the structure

```
|[ n: int
; "establish P0 for n = 0"
; do n ≠ N →
        {P0 ∧ n ≠ N}
        "modification of x"
        { P0ⁿₙ₊₁}
      ; n:= n + 1 {P0}
  od
]|
```

this has the pleasing consequence that the elements of f are involved in the computation one by one – namely in the order of increasing index.

The initialization is trivial: $x:= 0; n:= 0$.

For $\mathtt{modification\ of}$ x we elaborate $P0_{n+1}^{n}$:

$$0 \leq n + 1 \leq N \ \wedge \ x = (\underline{MIN}\ i, j: 0 \leq i \leq j \leq n + 1: Q(i, j))$$

The first term is a consequence of the precondition. Since

$$(0 \leq i \leq j \leq n + 1) \ \equiv \ (0 \leq i \leq j \leq n) \ \vee \ (0 \leq i \leq j = n + 1)$$

the second term can be rewritten as

$$
\begin{aligned}
x = \min \ &((\underline{MIN}\ i, j: 0 \leq i \leq j \leq n: Q(i, j)) \\
&(\underline{MIN}\ i: 0 \leq i \leq n + 1: Q(i, n + 1)))
\end{aligned}
$$

We know the first argument of $\min$ from P0; the second argument is new, however. It suggests the introduction of a new variable, for example y, and a new invariant P0 ∧ P1, where P1 is given by

$$P1: \quad y = (\underline{MIN}\ i: 0 \leq i \leq n: Q(i, n))$$

Provided that $P1_{n+1}^{n}$ already holds, the $\mathtt{modification\ of}$ x can be carried out by

$$x:= \min(x, y)$$

To establish $P1_{n+1}^{n}$ we elaborate this

$$
\begin{aligned}
y &= (\underline{MIN}\ i: 0 \leq i \leq n + 1: Q(i, n + 1)) \\
&= \min((\underline{MIN}\ i: 0 \leq i \leq n: Q(i, n + 1)), Q(n + 1, n + 1)) \\
&= \min((\underline{MIN}\ i: 0 \leq i \leq n: Q(i, n) + f(n)), 0) \\
&= \min((\underline{MIN}\ i: 0 \leq i \leq n: Q(i, n)) + f(n), 0)
\end{aligned}
$$

after which we recognize the expression from P1 in the first argument of min (in the last line). Thus we get the following structure for minsegsum:

```
|[ n, y: int; x:= 0; y:= 0; n := 0 {P0 ∧ P1}
; do n ≠ N  →  {n ≠ N ∧ P0 ∧ P1}
          y:= min(y + f(n), 0) {n ≠ N ∧ P0 ∧ P1ⁿ_{n+1}}
        ; x:= min(x, y) {n ≠ N ∧ P0ⁿ_{n+1} ∧ P1ⁿ_{n+1}}
        ; n:= n + 1 {P0 ∧ P1}
  od
]|
```

Eliminating the function min and exploiting the obvious invariant $x \leq 0$ gives the following solution for minsegsum (without annotation):

```
|[ n, y: int; x:= 0; y:= 0; n:= 0
; do n ≠ N  →   y:= y + f(n)
          ; if y ≥ 0  →  y:= 0
            [] y < 0  →   if x ≤ y  →  skip
                          [] x > y  →  x:= y
                          fi
            fi
          ; n:= n + 1
  od
]|
```

And this apparently concludes our discussion of minsegsum, as our solution requires a computation time proportional to N, and we have already decided that this is the most we can achieve. The strategy adopted has led to surprisingly efficient solutions before.

To start with, we introduce only P0 which describes what should be retained – here in the variable x – for the desired answer to be known upon completion. The required invariant of P0 poses a new problem, which in turn dictates which extra data from the past should also be retained; therefore P1 and y were introduced. That was sufficient this time; with more complicated programs it may be necessary to introduce the variables of the local state space in a larger number of steps.

The coincidence count

Given two integer sequences in monotonically increasing order, F(i: $0 \leq i < M$) and G(j: $0 \leq j < N$), the problem is to find the number of values occurring in both sequences. More precisely, we are looking for a solution for coincount, specified by

```
|[ M, N: int {M ≥ 0  ∧  N ≥ 0}
 ; F(i: 0 ≤ i < M), G(j: 0 ≤ j < N): array of int
   { (A i, j: 0 ≤ i < j < M: F(i) < F(j))  ∧
     (A i, j: 0 ≤ i < j < N: G(i) < G(j))}
 ; |[ k: int
    ; coincount
      {k = (N i, j: 0 ≤ i < M  ∧  0 ≤ j < N: F(i) = G(j))}
    ]|
 ]|
```

This is a canonic problem. We can regard the sequences F and G as the ordered representations of two sets of integers. In this terminology coincount determines the cardinality of the intersection of these two sets. (For the sake of simplicity coincount determines only the cardinality of the intersection; determination of the intersection itself would require only a simple addition.) Since determination of the intersection of two sets is a common problem, this short digression also explains the popularity of sorting routines.

If we do not want to disturb the symmetry, the standard method, 'replace constants by variables in the postcondition', leads to the introduction of two integer variables m and n and, for example, the invariant

```
P0:   0 ≤ m ≤ M  ∧  0 ≤ n ≤ N  ∧
      k = (N i, j: 0 ≤ i < m  ∧  0 ≤ j < n: F(i) = G(j))
```

Initialization is no problem, since the state $(k, m, n) = (0, 0, 0)$

satisfies PO, and PO is useful in the sense that, as evident from its construction, the postcondition follows from

PO ∧ m = M ∧ n = N

The point is, however, that when repeatedly incrementing m and/or n by 1, there are many paths that lead from (m, n) = (0, 0) to (m, n) = (M, N), so that the question is raised of whether we can successfully exploit this freedom by limiting it, i.e. by strengthening the invariant.

Let us, for example, try to choose the path from the point (m, n) such that each coincidence in the state F(m) = G(n) is detected. This means that in the state F(m) ≠ G(n) the increment of k is

(N̲ j: 0 ≤ j < n: F(m) = G(j)) = 0

when incrementing m by 1, a conclusion which is guaranteed, thanks to the monotonicity of G, by

F(m) > G(n − 1)

To achieve this, we strengthen PO – for reasons of symmetry with two terms – to P1:

P: PO ∧ F(m) > G(n − 1) ∧ G(n) > F(m − 1)

where F(−1) and G(−1) are in addition defined as 'minus infinity', and F(M) and G(N) as 'plus infinity'.

From this stronger P1 we gain the advantage that the computation need not be continued to (m, n) = (M, N), since

P1 ∧ (m = M ∨ n = N)

already implies the postcondition. (It follows from P1 ∧ m = M that G(n) > F(M − 1) so that G(j: n ≤ j < N) does not yield any coincidences, because of the monotonicity of both sequences; the same goes for P1 ∧ n = N.)

The invariance of G(n) > F(m − 1) implies that m:= m + 1 should be given G(n) > F(m) as a guard, and in this way we get the symmetric solution for coincount

```
|[ m, n: int
; k:= 0; m:= 0; n:= 0
; do m ≠ M ∧ n ≠ N →
       if  G(n) > F(m)  →  m:= m + 1
       ▯  G(n) = F(m)  →  k:= k + 1; m:= m + 1; n:= n + 1
```

$$\square \ G(n) \ < \ F(m) \ \rightarrow \ n\!:= \ n \ + \ 1$$
$$\underline{fi}$$
$$\underline{od}$$
$$]|$$

Seeing the simplicity of the eventual solution, the way that led to it is perhaps rather long. It can indeed be shortened. By way of introduction, first consider a one-dimensional count. With a postcondition

$$c = (\underline{N} \ i: 0 \leq i < M: F(i) = 7)$$

the standard strategy suggests the invariant

QO: $0 \leq m \leq M \ \wedge \ c = (\underline{N} \ i: 0 \leq i < m: F(i) = 7)$

By adding the 'missing part' to both sides of the equality sign, we get

Q1: $0 \leq m \leq M \ \wedge$
$$c + (\underline{N} \ i: m \leq i < M: F(i) = 7) =$$
$$(\underline{N} \ i: 0 \leq i < M: F(i) = 7)$$

Relations QO and Q1 are obviously equivalent.

Going back to coincount, instead of PO we could have chosen (compare Q1):

P2: $0 \leq m \leq M \ \wedge \ 0 \leq n \leq N \ \wedge$
$$k + (\underline{N} \ i, \ j: m \leq i < M \ \wedge \ n \leq j < N: F(i) = G(j)) =$$
$$(\underline{N} \ i, \ j: 0 \leq i < M \ \wedge \ 0 \leq j < N: F(i) = G(j))$$

Just as PO did not determine the path from point (m, n), neither does P2. The choice of the invariant P2, however, leads almost inevitably to the coincount already found.

If we had thought of P2 to start with, we would probably have preferred it to PO on account of the following consideration. If we initialize (with $k = 0$), then (without inspecting the sequences) $m = 0 \ \wedge \ n = 0$ is obligatory for P2; for PO, $m = 0 \ \vee \ n = 0$ suffices, a liberty which we did not exploit, partly to avoid disrupting the symmetry and partly because we would not have known how to exploit it.

In the end exactly the reverse is true: to be able to conclude the postcondition from PO, the additional condition $m = M \ \wedge \ n = N$ is required, whereas for P2 the weaker $m = M \ \vee \ n = N$ is sufficient. The weaker the required additional condition, the stronger the guard of the repetition, and the greater the probability for a quicker termination.

The moral of this story is that if on initializing we find ourselves with some freedom, we would probably do better to investigate whether we can successfully stick to another invariant.

EXERCISE

Generalize the given solution for coincount for the case in which the sequences are ascending, i.e.:

$$(A\ i,\ j: 0 \leq i < j < M: F(i) \leq F(j))\ \wedge$$
$$(A\ i,\ j: 0 \leq i < j < N: G(i) \leq G(j))$$

The minimum distance

Find a solution for mindist, specified by

```
|[ M, N: int {M ≥ 1 ∧ N ≥ 1}
; F(i: 0 ≤ i < M), G(j: 0 ≤ j < N): array of int
  { (A, i, j: 0 ≤ i < j < M: F(i) ≤ F(j)) ∧
    (A, i, j: 0 ≤ i < j < N: G(i) ≤ G(j)) ∧
    D = (MIN i, j: 0 ≤ i < M ∧ 0 ≤ j < N: abs(F(i) − G(j)))}
; |[ d: int
   ; mindist
     {d = D}
   ]|
]|
```

To begin with it would be good to define a (symbolic) minimum for an empty bag of integers as well; we choose 'plus infinity' for this, i.e. a value at least the looked for minimum over the non-empty bag. (In an analogous way the (symbolic) maximum for an empty bag is 'minus infinity'.) In this case we can, for example, choose:

```
max(F(M − 1) − G(0), G(N − 1) − F(0))
```

for 'plus infinity'.

Now that we have also defined a minimum for the empty bag, there are again two possibilities for the invariant. Because of the moral of the last example, we do *not* choose

```
d = (MIN i, j: 0 ≤ i < m ∧ 0 ≤ j < n: abs(F(i) − G(j)))
```

but

```
PO:  0 ≤ m ≤ M ∧ 0 ≤ n ≤ N ∧
     min(d, (MIN i, j: m ≤ i < M ∧ n ≤ j < N: abs(F(i) − G(j))))
     = D
```

86

Invariant PO holds in (d, m, n) = ("plus infinity", 0, 0), so that initialization is no problem. Furthermore, thanks to the introduction of the symbolic minimum over the empty bag, we have

PO ∧ (m = M ∨ n = N) ⇒ d = D

For $0 \leq m < M \land 0 \leq n < N$ we consider the following two cases.

F(m) ≥ G(n)

Writing the two arguments of min one under the other for the sake of clarity and denoting abs(F(i) − G(j)) by K(i, j):

```
min(d,
    (MIN i, j: m ≤ i < M ∧ n ≤ j < N: K(i, j))) =
min(d,
    min( (MIN i: m ≤ i < M: K(i, n)),
         (MIN i, j: m ≤ i < M ∧ n + 1 ≤ j < N: K(i, j)))) =
min(d,
    min(K(m, n),
        (MIN i, j: m ≤ i < M ∧ n + 1 ≤ j < N: K(i, j)))) =
min(min(d, K(m, n)),
    (MIN i, j: m ≤ i < M ∧ n + 1 ≤ j < N: K(i, j)))
```

In the above reduction the first equality sign is based on the definition of MIN; the second equality sign (also on the definition of K(i, j) on the inequality F(m) ≥ G(n) and on the monotonicity of the F sequence; and the third equality sign on the definition of min.

G(n) ≥ F(m)

For reasons of symmetry the treatment is analogous. Using the functions min and max, the above analysis leads to the following solution for mindist:

```
|[ m, n: int
; d:= max(F(M − 1) − G(0), G(N − 1) − F(0))
; m:= 0; n:= 0
; do m ≠ M ∧ n ≠ N →
      if F(m) ≥ G(n) →
            d:= min(d, F(m) − G(n)); n:= n + 1
      ▯ G(n) ≥ F(m) →
            d:= min(d, G(n) − F(m)); m:= m + 1
      fi
  od
]|
```

Rewriting without using the functions min and max is left to the reader.

Remark. For the reduction we used

    min(A, min(B, C)) = min(min(A, B), C)

If instead of the function notation we had used the infix operator min, this proposition would have been

    A min (B min C) = (A min B) min C

That is, the infix operator min is not only symmetric but also associative, and we could have written A min B min C. The same goes for max. In our reduction we have still used the function notation (one last time) for conventional reasons.   ■

The maximal monotone subsequence

Given a sequence $F(i: 0 \leq i < N)$, where $0 \leq N$, $F(i: k \leq i < k + h)$ is called a monotone subsequence of length h, if $Q(k, h)$ holds, where $Q(k, h)$ is given by

$$Q(k, h): \quad 0 \leq k \leq k + h \leq N \;\wedge$$
$$((\underline{A}\ i,\ j:\ k \leq i < j < k + h:\ F(i) \leq F(j))\ \vee$$
$$(\underline{A}\ i,\ j:\ k \leq i < j < k + h:\ F(i) \geq F(j)))$$

Give a program that determines the maximum length of some monotone subsequence for given F. Formally: write a program maxmonlen which satisfies the specification

```
|[ N: int {N ≥ 0}
 ; F(i: 0 ≤ i < N): array of int
 ; |[ q: int
   ; maxmonlen
      {q = (MAX k, h: Q(k, h): h)}
   ]|
 ]|
```

(With this example in particular, the independent reader is strongly advised *not* to read on, but to put the book aside and to try to construct a solution for maxmonlen. This advice is given because it is possible to learn only from one's experience how easy it is to make things unnecessarily difficult.)

Because of the way in which maxmonlen is specified, there are three snags – two small and one large.

The first little snag lies in the fact that the F sequence can also be empty. Not only must $q = 0$ hold for $N = 0$ upon completion, but $N = 0$ is also the only case in which this can hold upon completion since for positive N, q is at least 1. In general we always try to introduce as few special cases as possible and, if the case $N = 0$ can be smoothly taken along with the general case, this comes in useful. If in the general case $N = 0$

turns out to be a hindrance, we should remember that we can also deal with· it separately.

The second little snag is that N no longer occurs explicitly in our postcondition: it is stashed away as a global constant in the definition of $Q(k, h)$.

The big snag, however, is the following: according to the definition, a monotone subsequence is either ascending or descending or both. Moreover, we do not know if the maximal length is realized by an ascending or descending subsequence. Experience has taught us that it is very tempting to split sequence F into ascending, descending and constant trajectories. The great many ways in which they can succeed each other, however, leads to a combinatorial explosion. All this trouble can be avoided completely when the identifications of ascending and descending subsequences are kept strictly separated.

In order to carry out such a separation, we shall first confine ourselves to ascending subsequences, i.e. we consider the program whose postcondition is

$$q = (\underline{MAX}\ k, h: AS(k, h, N): h)$$

where AS is defined by

$$AS(k, h, n): \ 0 \le k \le k + h \le n \ \wedge$$
$$(\underline{A}\ i, j: k \le i < j < k + h: F(i) \le F(j))$$

In the meantime we have dealt with the second little snag by the introduction of n; for the sake of convenience we shall confine ourselves to $1 \le N$ from now on.

As invariant we choose

$$q = (\underline{MAX}\ k, h: AS(k, h, n): h) \ \wedge \ 1 \le n \le N$$

Since

$$(\underline{MAX}\ k, h: AS(k, h, n + 1): h) =$$
$$(\underline{MAX}\ k, h: AS(k, h, n): h)\ \underline{max}$$
$$(\underline{MAX}\ k, h: AS(k, h, n + 1) \ \wedge \ k + h = n + 1: h)$$

we maintain as additional invariant (compare the minimal segment sum),

$$v = (\underline{MAX}\ k, h: AS(k, h, n) \ \wedge \ k + h = n: h)$$

or, after elimination of k,

$$v = (\underline{MAX} \quad h: 0 \le n - h \le n \ \wedge$$
$$(\underline{A}\ i, j: n - h \le i < j < n: F(i) \le F(j)): h)$$

For the subproblem we get

```
|[ n, v: int
; n:= 1; q:= 1; v:= 1
; do n ≠ N → if  F(n) ≥ F(n − 1) →  v:= v + 1
                                    ; q:= q max v
             ▯ F(n) < F(n − 1) →  v:= 1
             fi ; n:= n + 1
  od
]|
```

a solution which does not work for $N = 0$.

After this there follows the solution for maxmonlen, where w is analogous to v:

```
if N = 0 →  q:= 0
▯ N > 0 →
   |[ n, v, w: int
   ; n:= 1; q:= 1; v:= 1; w:= 1
   ; do n ≠ N →
         if F(n) > F(n − 1) →  w:= 1; v:= v + 1
         ▯ F(n) = F(n − 1) →  w:= w + 1; v:= v + 1
         ▯ F(n) < F(n − 1) →  w:= w + 1; v:= 1
         fi
       ; q:= q max v max w
       ; n:= n + 1
     od
   ]|
fi
```

With

```
if q ≥ v ∧ q ≥ w → skip
▯ q < v ∨ q < w →
        if v ≥ w → q:= v ▯ w ≥ v → q:= w fi
fi
```

the infix operator max can be eliminated, if so desired.

The inversion count

We consider two sequences of natural numbers $X(i: 0 \leq i < N)$ and $Y(i: 0 \leq i < N)$ which satisfy the following relation:

- $X(i: 0 \leq i < N)$ is a permutation of the numbers from 0 through $N - 1$ $\land$
- $(\underline{A} \ j: 0 \leq j < N: (\underline{N} \ i: 0 \leq i < j: X(i) < X(j)) = Y(j))$

Remark. Formally we could also have expressed the first term of this relation by

$$(\underline{A} \ j: 0 \leq j < N: (\underline{N} \ i: 0 \leq i < N: X(i) = j) = 1) \qquad \blacksquare$$

EXERCISE

Verify that it follows from the above that:

$$(\underline{A} \ j: 0 \leq j < N: Y(j) \leq j)$$

For such a pair of sequences invercount is specified by

```
|[ N: int {N ≥ 0}
 ; |[ v(i: 0 ≤ i < N): array of int
      {v = X}
    ; invercount
      {v = Y}
    ]|
 ]|
```

An observation that brings relief is that any natural number is equal to the number of smaller natural numbers, i.e. $(\underline{N} \ i:: 0 \leq i$

$< n$) $= n$ for $n \geq 0$. From this $X(N - 1) = Y(N - 1)$ follows, i.e. the value of $v(N - 1)$ is left unchanged by invercount. This suggests we should make the elements of v equal to those of Y in 'back-to-front' order. As invariant we choose P0 ∧ P1 ∧ P2 where:

> P0: $v(i: 0 \leq i < n)$ is a permutation of the numbers from 0 through $n - 1$
>
> P1: $(\underline{A} j: 0 \leq j < n: (\underline{N} i: 0 \leq i < j: v(i) < v(j)) = Y(j))$
>
> P2: $(\underline{A} j: n \leq j < N: v(j) = Y(j))$

The invariant follows from $v = X$ ∧ $n = N$, $v = Y$ follows from P2 ∧ $n = 0$.

The decrement of $n := n - 1$ does not disturb P2 on the basis of the relief-bringing observation, and leaves P1 trivially unchanged; P0, however, will generally be disturbed: after decrementing n, $v(i: 0 \leq i < n)$ is a permutation of the numbers from 0 through $v(n) - 1$ and from $v(n) + 1$ through n. By decrementing these latter numbers by 1, we restore P0 without disturbing P1 ∧ P2. For invercount we find

```
|[ n: int; n:= N
; do n ≠ 0 →
      |[ i: int; i:= 0; n:= n - 1
      ; do  i ≠ n →  if  v(i) > v(n)  →  v:(i)= v(i) - 1
                     []  v(i) < v(n)  →  skip
                     fi; i:= i + 1
         od
      ]|
   od
]|
```

There are N! different values possible for X. The property mentioned in the exercise also allows N! different values for Y. If they are all possible – as is indeed the case – it means that the execution of invercount does not destroy any information, and that therefore there is also a program which, given the Y sequence, reconstructs the corresponding X sequence. The transformation of v, realized by the execution of invercount, is then invertible.

Any deterministic program S, whose execution does not destroy information, has an inverse S^{-1}. Whether a text for S^{-1} can be derived directly from the one for S depends on the way in which S is programmed. The solution for invercount given above was carefully chosen in such a way that invercount^{-1} can be derived from it.

The following annotated statements, given in two columns, are each other's inversion:

```
x:= x + 1              x:= x - 1
S0; S1                 S1⁻¹; S0⁻¹
|[ x: int              |[ x: int
 ; x:= exp1             ; x:= exp2
 ; S                    ; S⁻¹
    {x = exp2}             {x = exp1}
]|                     ]|
if B0 → S0 {C0}        if C1 → S1⁻¹ {B1}
 ▯ B1 → S1 {C1}         ▯ C0 → S0⁻¹ {B0}
fi                     fi
where ¬(B0 ∧ B1)  and  ¬(C0 ∧ C1)
{¬C}                   {¬B}
do B → S {C} od        do C → S⁻¹ {B} od
{¬B}                   {¬C}
```

We shall now annotate invercount in such a way that the inversion rules mentioned above are applicable:

```
|[ n: int; n:= N
   {n = N}
 ; do n ≠ 0 →
         |[ i: int; i:= 0; n:= n - 1
            {i = 0}
          ; do i ≠ n →
                  if v(i) > v(n) → v:(i)= v(i) - 1 {v(i) ≥ v(n)}
                   ▯ v(i) < v(n) → skip {v(i) < v(n)}
                  fi; i:= i + 1 {i ≠ 0}
              od
              {i = n}
         ]| {n ≠ N}
   od
   {n = 0}
]|
```

The functional specification for invercount⁻¹ is:

```
|[ N: int {N ≥ 0}
 ; |[ v(i: 0 ≤ i < N): array of int
      {v = Y}
    ; invercount⁻¹
      {v = X}
   ]|
]|
```

It is satisfied by the unannotated inverse of invercount:

```
|[ n: int; n:= 0
 ; do n ≠ N →
```

```
|[ i: int; i:= n
; do  i ≠ 0  →   i:= i - 1
                 ; if  v(i) < v(n)  →  skip
                   [] v(i) ≥ v(n)  →  v:(i) = v(i) + 1
                   fi
       od; n:= n + 1
   ]|
 od
]|
```

EXERCISE

Annotate this solution for invercount^{-1}, so that its inverse yields invercount again.

Remark. Program inversion was developed by coincidence (as a kind of programming joke, resulting from the above problems, which together once served as examination questions). Later program inversion became applicable to serious program development when in a program in which, for relatively complicated, recurrently defined F, $f = F(q)$ was added as invariant for efficiency reasons. The only changes to which q was subjected were $q:= q + 1$ and $q:= q - 1$; for the corresponding, relatively complicated modifications of the value of f, one could be obtained by inversion from the other.   ∎

Numbers with factors 2, 3 and 5 only

Give a program that generates in increasing order the first 1000 solutions of the equation in x:

$$(\underline{E}\ n2, n3, n5: n2 \geq 0\ \wedge\ n3 \geq 0\ \wedge\ n5 \geq 0: 2^{n2} \cdot 3^{n2} \cdot 5^{n5} = x)$$

Another way to characterize the set V of solutions of this equation is:

(i)   1 belongs to V;
(ii)   if x belongs to V, then $2 \cdot x$, $3 \cdot x$ and $5 \cdot x$ also belong to V;
(iii) only values which belong to V on the basis of (i) and (ii) belong to V.

Let $V1000(i: 0 \leq i < 1000)$ be the increasing sequence of the smallest 1000 elements of V. The functional specification of hamming (so called after R.W. Hamming who launched this programming problem) is then

```
|[ |[ x(i: 0 ≤ i < 1000): array of int
   ; hamming
     {x = V1000}
   ]|
]|
```

The invariant is obviously

PO: $1 \leq n \leq 1000\ \wedge\ (\underline{A}\ i: 0 \leq i < n: V1000(i) = x(i))$

which can easily be initialized for $n = 1$ on the basis of (i). For hamming this suggests a solution of the structure

96

```
|[ n: int
; x:(0)= 1; n:= 1 {P0}
; do n ≠ 1000 → "increment n by 1 under invariance of P0"
  od
]|
```

The command to increment n by 1 under invariance of P0 means that the value of V1000(n) must be determined. On the basis of (ii) and (iii) V1000(n) is of the form 2 · x(i2) with 0 ≤ i2 < n, or of the form 3 · x(i3) with 0 ≤ i3 < n, or of the form 5 · x(i5) with 0 ≤ i5 < n. Note that since 2 · x, 3 · x and 5 · x are all larger than x, membership on the basis of (ii) always depends on a *smaller* x which belongs to V. This is the property that enables us to generate elements of V in increasing order.)

Of the numbers of the form 2 · x(i2), 3 · x(i3) and 5 · x(i5), we need the smallest one that is > x(n − 1). In other words, we must have the minimum of the smallest one > x(n − 1) of the form 2 · x(i2), of the smallest one > x(n − 1) of the form 3 · x(i3), and of the smallest one > x(n − 1) of the form 5 · x(i5).

For the *smallest* one of the form 2 · x(i2) that is > x(n − 1), the values 2 · x(i2) must be investigated in *increasing* order – see the Linear Search. Since 2 · x is a monotonically increasing function of x, and since x(i: 0 ≤ i < n) is increasing, this means that the values 2 · x(i2) can be investigated in order of increasing i2. The same observation holds for the other two factors and in this way we find for hamming:

```
|[ n: int
; x:(0)= 1; n:= 1
; do n ≠ 1000 →
      |[ i2, i3, i5: int
      ; i2:= 0; i3:= 0; i5:= 0
      ; do 2 * x(i2) ≤ x(n − 1)  →  i2:= i2 + 1 od
      ; do 3 * x(i3) ≤ x(n − 1)  →  i3:= i3 + 1 od
      ; do 5 * x(i5) ≤ x(n − 1)  →  i5:= i5 + 1 od
      ; x:(n)= (2*x(i2)) min  (3*x(i3)) min (5*x(i5))
      ; n:= n + 1
      ]|
  od
]|
```

This does not mean that we are finished, however. The only function of the assignment i2:= 0 is to realize the invariant of the next linear search. Since the sequence x is increasing, this invariant at the end of the inner block is not disturbed by n:= n + 1. The invariant of the linear search is also a possible invariant of the outer repetition, provided we take the declaration and initialization of i2 'outside'. *Mutatis mutandis* the same holds for i3 and i5, and thus we get the following solution for hamming:

```
|[ n, i2, i3, i5: int
; x:(0)= 1; n:= 1; i2:= 0; i3:= 0; i5:= 0
; do n ≠ 1000  →
        do 2 * x(i2) ≤ x(n − 1)  →   i2:= i2 + 1 od
      ; do 3 * x(i3) ≤ x(n − 1)  →   i3:= i3 + 1 od
      ; do 5 * x(i5) ≤ z(n − 1)  →   i5:= i5 + 1 od
      ; x:(n)=
         (2*x(i2)) min  (3*x(i3)) min (5*x(i5))
       ; n:= n + 1
    od
]|
```

EXERCISE

Demonstrate that, contrary to the first solution for hamming, the repetitive statement

```
do 2 * x(i2) ≤ x(n − 1) → i2:= i2 + 1 od
```

in the last solution for hamming could be replaced by the alternative statement

```
if 2 * x(i2) ≤ x(n − 1)  →   i2:= i2 + 1
 0 2 * x(i2) > x(n − 1)  →   skip
fi
```

Mutatis mutandis the same holds for the next two repetitive statements.

The transition from the first solution to the second solution is a standard transformation, known as 'taking a relation outside a repetition'. In fact, it is so much a standard that in such a case an experienced programmer does not even bother to write down the first version, but immediately asks with which auxiliary variables in the block surrounding the repetition one iteration could profit from the preceding one. (This more direct way is the one followed at the introduction of y when developing minsegsum.)

Coordinate transformation

Earlier (see p. 55) we considered square root, specified by

```
|[ N: int {N ≥ 0}
; |[ a: int
   ; square root
      {a² ≤ N  ∧  (a + 1)² > N}
   ]|
]|
```

We then came up with the solution

```
|[ b: int
; a:= 0; b:= 1
; do b * b ≤ N  →  b:= 2 * b od
; do b ≠ a + 1  →
      |[ c: int; c:= (a + b)div 2
      ; if c * c ≤ N  →  a:= c
         ▯ c * c > N  →  b:= c
        fi
      ]|
   od
]|
```

This solution was quite efficient in the sense that the number of iterations of the repetition was proportional to log N, and not proportional to $\sqrt{N}$ as in an earlier solution. In this solution, each iteration requires a multiplication, however, and since on the whole the general multiplicative operation requires (an order of magnitude) more time than additive operations, halvings and doublings, the question arises whether these general multiplications can be eliminated. This can indeed be done; we shall carry out the elimination in a number of steps.

We have already noted that the difference $b - a$ is always a power of 2, and that the div 2 could therefore be replaced by / 2. We do this and, at the same time, maintain the invariant $d = b - a$.

```
|[ b, d: int
; a:= 0; b:= 1; d:= 1
; do b * b ≤ N   →   b:= 2 * b; d:= 2 * d od
; do b ≠ a + 1   →
        |[ c: int; c:= (a + b)/ 2
        ; if c * c ≤ N   →   a:= c; d:= d / 2
           ▯ c * c > N   →   b:= c; d:= d / 2
           fi
        ]|
  od
]|
```

The inner block is equivalent to

```
|[ c: int; c:= (a + b)/ 2; d:= d / 2
   {a + d = c  ∧  c + d = b}
; if  c² ≤ N   →   a:= c
   ▯ c² > N   →   b:= c
   fi
]|
```

(For the sake of convenience we have permitted ourselves the exponent for now.)

We can replace all four cs by (a + d) in the last alternative statement, but then the local c is not used at all any more and can be left out with impunity. The inner block is thus reduced to

```
d:= d / 2
; if (a + d)² ≤ N   →   a:= a + d
   ▯ (a + d)² > N   →   b:= a + d
   fi
```

Next we observe that in the first repetition the invariant $a = 0$ implies $b = d$, thus the guard $b^2 \leq N$ has the same value as $d^2 \leq N$, and can be replaced by it.

Next we observe that, because of the invariant $d = b - a$ of the second repetition, the guard $b \neq a + 1$ has the same value as $d \neq 1$, and can thus be replaced by it. But then the variable b can be left out with impunity. The result of all these substitutions and omissions is

```
|[ d: int
; a:= 0; d:= 1
; do d² ≤ N   →   d:= 2 * d od
; do d ≠ 1   →   d:= d / 2
                ; if (a + d)² ≤ N   →   a:= a + d
                   ▯ (a + d)² > N   →   skip
                   fi
  od
]|
```

This was only a first step, to enable us to rewrite the guard $(a + d)^2 \leq N$ as $2 \cdot a \cdot d + d^2 \leq N - a^2$ – a form which suggests the introduction of three variables, p, q and r, which satisfy

$$p = a \cdot d \wedge q = d^2 \wedge r = N - a^2$$

This leads to the following program. (Note that because of $a = 0$ in the first repetition, doubling d does not necessarily involve a doubling of p.)

```
|[ p, q, r, d: int
; p:= 0; q:= 1; r:= N; a:= 0; d:= 1
; do d² ≤ N  →  q:= 4 * q; d:= 2 * d od
; do d ≠ 1  →  q:= q / 4; p:= p / 2; d:= d / 2
              ; if  2 * a * d + d² ≤ N − a² →   r:= r − (2 * a * d + d²)
                                           ; p:= p + q; a:= a + d
               ▯ 2 * a * d + d² > N − a² →   skip
               fi
  od {a = p}
]|
```

In the first repetition the value of the guard $d^2 \leq N$ is equal to that of $q \leq r$, by which it may be replaced.

In the second repetition the value of the guard $d \neq 1$ is equal to that of $q \neq 1$, by which it may be replaced.

In the alternative construction the value of $2 \cdot a \cdot d + d^2$ is equal to that of $2 \cdot p + q$, by which it may be replaced, and that of $N - a^2$ is equal to that of r.

By these substitutions d is made superfluous, and the assignments to a can be left out, provided that we insert $a := p$ at the end.

For the sake of brevity the auxiliary variable h, which satisfies $h = 2 \cdot p + q$, is introduced:

```
|[ p, q, r: int
; p:= 0; q:= 1; r:= N
; do q ≤ r  →  q:= 4 * q od
; do q ≠ 1  →
     |[ h: int
     ; q:= q / 4; h:= p + q; p:= p / 2
     ; if  h ≤ r  →  r:= r − h; p:= p + q
        ▯ h > r  →  skip
       fi
     ]|
  od; a:= p
]|
```

Remark. In a microprogrammed binary machine, extraction of roots should not take much more time than division with this algorithm.   ∎

Here we have shown extensively the transformation process – introduction of new variables and invariants, rewriting guards, and then elimination of original variables. Carried out this way it requires a lot of writing. Someone who is used to this method of program development would make the transition from old to new variables in one step, without writing down the version with both variables. Rewriting, which this method of program development entails, remains a drawback, however.

On account of a directed graph

We consider a graph with N different nodes, numbered from 0 through N − 1, and M directed branches. Any branch has one of the N nodes as starting point and one of the N nodes as end point. A branch is called an 'outgoing branch' of its starting point and an 'incoming branch' of its end point. The end point of a branch is said to be 'directly reachable' from the starting point of that branch.

The structure of such a graph can be fixed in various ways. The most symmetric is by means of two sequences, $s(i: 0 \leq i < M)$ and $e(i: 0 \leq i < M)$, such that $s(i)$ and $e(i)$ are the numbers of the starting point and the end point, respectively, of the ith branch (in some arbitrary numbering). This representation may be symmetric, but it is not very practicable for most applications: in order to determine which nodes are directly reachable from node k, the whole s sequence must be searched to determine the values of i for which $s(i) = k$ holds.

We can order the branches: first the outgoing branches of node 0, then the outgoing branches of node 1, etc.; branches with the same starting point can then again be ordered by ascending numbers of their end points. By means of this ordering the information in the s sequence can also be represented by the sequence $from(j: 0 \leq j < N + 1)$ such that

        (A j:0 ≤ j < N:
          (A i: from(j) ≤ i < from(j + 1):
            node e(i) is directly reachable from node j))

The sequences from and e fix the structure of the graph.

EXERCISE

Verify $from(0) = 0$ and $from(N) = M$; also check that $from(j + 1) - from(j) =$ the number of outgoing branches of node j.

If a graph G is thus described by the sequences from and e, OUT(G, from, e) holds. The pair (from, e) quickly answers the question of which nodes are directly reachable from a node k.

This representation does not offer any help in finding from which nodes a node k is directly reachable. If this question is frequently asked, the complementary representation is chosen. In this representation the branches are ordered differently: first the incoming branches of node 0, then the incoming branches of node 1, etc., and branches with the same end point in order of ascending number of their starting points. The information contained in the e sequence can then be represented by the sequence to($j: 0 \le j < N + 1$) such that

```
(A j:0 ≤ j < N:
   (A i: to(j) ≤ i < to(j + 1):
      from node s(i) nodes j is directly reachable))
```

The sequences s and to then also fix the structure of the graph; if a graph G is described according to this convention, IN(G, b, to) holds.

Now design a program which, taking a representation of a graph G, can form the complementary representation.

```
|[ M, N: int {M ≥ 0 ∧ N ≥ 1}
; from(j: 0 ≤ j < N + 1), e(i: 0 ≤ i < M): array of int
  {OUT(G, from, e)}
; |[ b(i: 0 ≤ i < M), to(j: 0 ≤ j < N + 1): array of int
   ; graphcomplement
      {IN(G, b, to)}
   ]|
]|
```

A solution for graphcomplement will be given before its explanation.

```
|[ i, j: int
; j:= 0; do j ≠ N → to:(j)= 0; j:= j + 1 od
; i:= 0; do i ≠ M → to:(e(i))= to(e(i)) + 1; i:= i + 1 od
; to:(N)= M; j:= N
; do j ≠ 0 → j:= j - 1; to:(j)= to(j + 1) - to(j) od
; |[ q(j: 0 ≤ j < N): array of int
   ; j:= 0; do j ≠ N → q:(j)= to(j); j:= j + 1 od
   ; i:= 0; j:= 0
   ; do j ≠ N → {from(j) = i}
            do i < from(j + 1) →
                     b:(q(e(i)))= j
                   ; q:(e(i))= q(e(i)) + 1
                   ; i:= i + 1
```

```
            od ;    j:= j + 1
        od
    ]|
]|
```

Contrary to our habit, we shall not formulate any invariants for this program: it is somewhat laborious to formulate the invariant of the last repetition, and it does not really help in developing the program.

We know that eventually $to(j + 1) - to(j)$ equals the number of incoming branches of node j, but this is equal to the number of times that the value j occurs in the e sequence. In other words, the value of to can be computed from the e sequence, and the value of $from$ does not play any part in this. In the first two repetitions the counts are executed so that $t(j)$ equals the number of incoming branches of node j. After supplementing this with $to(N) = M$, to is given its eventual value by subtraction in the third repetition.

It becomes more complicated in the next inner block in which the value of $from$ must be involved in the computation, and b must be computed: if the branches are introduced in the computation in the order given (by $from$ and e), their starting points will end up in b all disordered. In order to avoid this, the local array q is introduced: $q(h)$ is the index in array b for the number of the starting point of the 'next' incoming branch of node h; in the program $h = e(i)$. Array q is initialized with the first N elements of to; each time a new element of b is defined by being indexed $q(h)$, this $q(h)$ is increased by 1.

In the last repetition i is the number (in the original order) of the current branch; i increases from 0 through M. The value of j, increasing from 0 through N, is always the number of the starting point of the current branch, so it is always the value of j which is filled in in b. The position (index) where this is done depends on the end point of the current branch, that is, on $e(i)$; in fact it is $q(e(i))$.

It now remains for us to synchronize the increment of i and j suitably. The formula at the bottom of p. 103 tells us exactly which successive i values correspond to each value of j. The outer repetition has a fixed number N of iterations, and at each iteration i is incremented by as many steps as necessary. The annotation $\{from(j) = i\}$ is a piece of the invariant of the outer repetition.

Remark. The convention that branches with the same starting point were ordered by end point was superfluous. It was useful for the sake of symmetry: thanks to array q, branches with the same end point are ordered by starting point upon completion. ■

Note that incrementing and decrementing by 1 are about the only arithmetic operations in this program. (Designers of machines would do well not to underestimate the importance of indexing compared with that of arithmetic.)

The shortest path

Consider a directed graph with N nodes, numbered from 0 through $N - 1$, and M branches, where each branch has a positive length. The graph is given (see p. 103) by array from$(j: 0 \leq j < N + 1)$, array e$(i: 0 \leq i < M)$ and array d$(i: 0 \leq i < M)$, such that:

```
(A j: 0 ≤ j < N:
   (A i: from(j) ≤ i < from(j + 1):
              node e(i) is directly reachable from
              node j via a branch of length d(i)))
```

A sequence of branches, such that for any successive pair the end point of the first is the starting point of the second, is called a **path** from the starting point of the first branch to the end point of the last branch of the sequence. A single branch is also a path; empty paths are also permitted when the starting point and end point of the path coincide.

The length of the path is defined as the sum of the lengths of the branches constituting the path. Write a program that determines a shortest path from node A to node B.

$$* \qquad * \qquad *$$

For the sake of brevity we shall call the length of a shortest path from A to X the 'distance from X', and we shall confine ourselves for now to the determination of the distance from B. The extra administration enabling a path to be known upon completion will come later.

If a shortest path from A to B goes via C, it begins with a shortest path from A to C. This would suggest determining the distances for the nodes of a graph in order of ascending distance. Let us call the nodes whose distance has been determined the black nodes. As soon as B is black, we have found the answer; if it turns out that the set of black nodes can no longer be extended before B is black, then B is not reachable from A.

How can the set of black nodes be extended? Only with a node that is not yet black but which is directly reachable from a black node: of

107

the non-black nodes, we are looking for one with the minimum distance. We colour the non-black nodes that are directly reachable from a black node grey; the remaining nodes are white.

If there are no grey nodes, the set of black nodes cannot be extended. If there are grey nodes, which do we then choose to make black? The shortest paths from A to a non-black node contain at least one branch from black to grey, and all preceding branches are from black to black. A path from A, starting with 0 or more branches from black to black and ending with one branch from black to grey, is called a 'special path' of its end point. A grey node with the shortest special path can be made black, and the length of this shortest special path is then the distance from B.

So it suffices to register for each grey node the length of its shortest special path. We consider the case that node C turns from grey to black. There are then three possibilities:

(i)   An outgoing branch of C leads to a white node. This node becomes grey, and the length of its minimal special path becomes the distance from C plus the length of the branch involved.

(ii) An outgoing branch of C leads to a grey node. The length of the minimal special path of this grey node becomes the minimum of what it was and the distance from C plus the length of the branch involved.

(iii) An outgoing branch of C leads to a black node. This branch is never part of a shortest path from A, and can be ignored.

We now have to ask ourselves what information we should store. On the one hand we want to be able speedily to compute the answer to common questions such as 'what is the colour of node X?'; on the other hand, keeping this information up to date must not be too laborious.

To record the colour we suggest an array $clr(i: 0 \le i < N)$ and the convention:

- $clr(i) = 0 \equiv$ node i is white,
- $clr(i) = 1 \equiv$ node i is grey,
- $clr(i) = 2 \equiv$ node i is black

With this, given the node number, neither checking nor changing the colour of the nodes is laborious.

For black nodes we must record the distance; for grey nodes we must register the length of the minimal special path. Since at the transition from grey to black the latter becomes the former, we represent these in the same array $dist(i: 0 \le i < N)$:

$$\text{dist}(i) = \text{undefined if } clr(i) = 0,$$
$$= \text{the length of the minimal special path of node } i \text{ if } clr(i) = 1,$$
$$= \text{the distance from node } i \text{ if } clr(i) = 2$$

In order to determine the distance our last task is to determine a grey node with a special path of minimal length. It is among the grey nodes in clr; extraction of this from clr, however, requires that the whole of the array clr is searched, and since the number of grey nodes is generally an order of magnitude smaller than N, it is desirable to speed up the identification of the grey nodes by means of some extra 'red tape'; this can be done by means of the integer variable grn and array gr(i: $0 \le i < N$) and the convention

gr(i: $0 \le i < grn$) = the sequence of numbers of the grey nodes (in some order or other)

Array gr and counter grn are changed when the collection of grey nodes changes:

● node k turns from white to grey:

gr: (grn) = k; grn:= grn + 1

● node gr(h) turns from grey to black:

grn:= grn − 1; gr:(h)= gr(grn)

Finally, we consider the extra information necessary for keeping track of the shortest path from A to B. Since we try to let the set of black nodes grow until it contains B, an obvious procedure is to record a shortest path from A to X for all black nodes X, and analogously a shortest path from A to X for any grey node X.

If a shortest (special) path from A to X ends with the branch from C to X, it suffices, as far as X is concerned, to register for X that it is preceded by C, provided that a shortest path is known for C.

This predecessor administration is kept in the array pred(i: $0 \le i < N$) for all grey and all black nodes with the exception of A, which does not have a predecessor. This does not matter because the shortest path from A to A is known: it is the empty path.

Finally we state, in more detail than in the formal specification, how the answer must be recorded.

K = 0 if B is not reachable from A
= the number of nodes on the shortest path found

and furthermore, if K $\ge$ 1,

L = the length of the shortest path found
PATH(i: 0 ≤ i < K) = the nodes on the shortest path found, in
order, starting with A and ending with B

From the formal specification we give the declaration:

```
|[ A, B, N, M: int
; from(j: 0 ≤ j < N + 1), e, d(i: 0 ≤ i < M: array of int
; |[ K, L: int
   ; PATH(i: 0 ≤ i < N): array of int
   ; shorpath
   ]|
]|
```

The essence of shorpath follows below; followed by a simple coda
on p. 111, in which the answer to the desired presentation is provided by
means of the variables K, L and PATH. (Note that at first the path is
constructed back to front.)

The initialization for the main repetition consists of making all
nodes white, followed by colouring A grey – with due regard to all
conventions. The main repetition terminates when all the grey nodes are
finished, or when B is black; note that both may be the case.

The inner block consists of three parts:

(i)   The selection of the grey node C which is to become black; variable
        h is introduced because C must be removed from gr(i: 0 ≤
        i < grn), variable min plays its usual part.

(ii)   Node C is made black, with due regard to the conventions.

(iii)   The outgoing branches of C are considered in turn; X is the end
        point of such a branch, len is the length of the shortest path from A
        ending with branch CX. Note that X and len are local constants;
        they have been introduced for the sake of brevity and for clarity.
        The alternative statement is exactly according to the analysis on
        p. 108; if the guard clr(X) = 1 is replaced by clr(X) ≥ 1, the
        alternative with the guard clr(X) = 2 can be dropped.

```
|[ grn, i: int
; clr, dist, gr, pred(j: 0 ≤ j < N): array of int
; i:= 0; do i ≠ N → clr:(i)= 0; i:= i + 1 od
; clr:(A)= 1; dist:(A)= 0 gr:(0)= A; grn:= 1
; do grn > 0 ∧ clr(B) ≠ 2 →
```

```
|[ h, min, C: int
; h:= 0; min:= dist(gr(0)); i:= 1
; do  i ≠ grn →
        if  dist(gr(i)) ≧ min  →  skip
        [] dist(gr(i)) ≦ min  →
              min:= dist(gr(i)); h:= i
      fi ; i:= i + 1
    od; C:= gr(h)
; clr:(C)= 2; grn:= grn− 1; gr:(h)= gr(grn)
; i:= from (C)
; do  i < from(C + 1)  →
        |[ X, len: int
        ; X:= e(i); len:= dist(C) + d(i)
        ; if  clr(X) = 0  →
                clr:(X)= 1; gr:(grn)= X; grn:= grn + 1
              ; dist:(X)= len
              ; pred:(x)= C
          [] clr(X) = 1  →
                if  len ≧ dist(X)  →  skip
                [] len ≦ dist(X)  →
                      dist:(X)= len
                    ; pred:(X)= C
              fi
          [] clr(X) = 2  →  skip
          fi; i:= i + 1
        ]|
      od
    ]|
  od
; if  clr(B) ≠ 2  →  K:= 0
  [] clr(B) = 2  →
      PATH:(0)= B; K:= 1
    ; do PATH(K − 1) ≠ A  →
            PATH:(K)= pred(PATH(K − 1)); K:= K + 1
        od
    ; |[ j: int; i:= 0; j:= K − 1
      ; do  i < j  →  PATH :swap(i, j)
                    ; i:= i + 1; j:= j − 1
          od
      ]|
    ; L:= dist(B)
  fi
]|
```

Remark. Variable i is used only in disjunct repetitions. We could have made inner blocks of those repetitions, each with a declaration of its 'own i'. That would have been very nice, but was not done out of laziness and (bad?) habit.   ∎

The binary search

The aim is to determine whether a given value occurs in a sorted sequence. More precisely, we are looking for a solution for search, specified by

```
|[ N: int {N > 0}
; W(i: 0 ≤ i > N): array of int
    {(A i, j: 0 ≤ i < j < N: W(i) ≤ W(j))}
; X: int
; |[ present: bool
    ; search
        {present ≡ (E i: 0 ≤ i < N: W(i) = X)}
    ]|
]|
```

If X does indeed occur in sequence W, it is unlikely that we can determine this without also finding out where X occurs in the sequence W, that is, without determining an i such that

W(i) = X

This relation is too strong to head for, since X does not necessarily occur in sequence W; if X does not occur in the sequence, i can at best denote where X should have been, that is,

W(i) < X < W(i + 1)

Since we do not know what is what, we head for

W(i) ≤ X < W(i + 1)

This relation is still a bit too strong, as X could be very large or very small. Having already upset the symmetry, we can deal with these two extreme cases in different ways. For very large X we extend the sequence W in our minds, i.e. in the relations, but not in the program itself, with a symbolic extra element $W(N)$ = 'plus infinity'; for very large X our inequalities are then satisfied for $i = N - 1$. For very small X we weaken our relation to

R: $W(i) \leq X < W(i + 1) \vee Q$

where Q is given by

Q: $(\underline{A}\ i: 0 \leq i < N: W(i) > X)$

By now R is so weak that as an equation in i it always has a solution, but even so, it is still strong enough to establish the postcondition quite simply. Once R holds,

present:= $W(i) = X$

assigns the desired value to present, because the sequence W is ascending.
From R we derive the invariant

P: $0 \leq i < j \leq N \wedge (W(i) \leq X < W(j) \vee Q)$

Initialization is no problem, because relation P holds for $(i, j) = (0, N)$; according to its construction, R follows from P $\wedge\ j = i + 1$.
Summing up the analysis so far, we get a solution of the following structure for **search**:

```
|[ i, j: int
; i:= 0; j:= N {P}
; do  j ≠ i + 1 →
            "decrement the difference j - 1 under invariance of P"
  od {R}
; present:= W(i) = X
]|
```

We shall now consider how, with the precondition P $\wedge\ j \neq i + 1$, we can reduce the difference $j - i$ under invariance of P. On this precondition there is an integer h such that $i < h < j$. With such an h the difference $j - i$ is reduced both by i:= h and by j:= h. The choice between these two possibilities is then determined by the requirement that P remain invariant. Elaborating P_h^i or P_h^j, respectively, leads to the guards in

if $W(h) \leq X \rightarrow$ i:= h ▯ $X < W(h) \rightarrow$ j:= h fi

It only remains to choose h. It is true that $i < h < j$ is established with h:= $i + 1$ or h:= $j - 1$, but there is a chance that a large difference

$j - i$ is only decremented by 1: this would lead to a search which would require N iterations in the worst case. The choice of $h := (i + j)\underline{div}\ 2$ would be much better: by this the difference $j - i$ is practically halved at each iteration, which guarantees a number of iterations proportional to $\log N$.

Thus we come to our eventual solution:

```
|[ i, j: int
; i:= 0; j:= N {P}
; do  j ≠ i + 1  →
      |[ h: int
      ; h:= (i + j)div 2 {i < h < j}
      ; if W(h) ≤ X  →  i:= h {P}
         ▯ X < W(h)  →  j:= h {P}
        fi {P}
      ]| {P}
  od {R}
; present:= W(i) = X
]|
```

Remarks.

(0)   The fact that the sequence W is sorted need not be involved in the derivation until assigning to present. Many a treatment in the literature is marred by the selection of an invariant for the repetition in which the fact that W is sorted is extensively involved; this leads to an unnecessarily laborious correctness proof.

(1)   Note that the termination proof of the repetition is completely independent of W and of X. If the alternative statement had been

$$\underline{if}\ \text{true} \to i := h\ \ ▯\ \ \text{true} \to j := h\ \underline{fi}$$

the repetition would still terminate.

(2)   Note that the correctness of our solution does not depend on whether div is rounded up or down, if rounding is necessary. We are completely at liberty, therefore, to replace the assignment to h by

$$h := i + (j - i)\underline{div}\ 2$$

a version which should possibly be preferred with a view to minimizing the chance of arithmetic overflow. Versions in which termination depends critically on rounding conventions are unfortunately not unusual in the literature.

(3)   The literature includes many versions in which the repetition can be terminated 'prematurely'. In fact, this amounts to strengthening one's guard to

$$j \neq i + 1\ \wedge\ W(i) \neq X$$

This so-called 'speeding-up' does not count for much, however. If X does occur in the sequence W, the expectation value of the gain is one iteration, otherwise nil. Each iteration, however, is more complicated. It is not easy to gain a little extra on a logarithmic algorithm!

(4)   Variable j, which is used only to establish r, in which it does not occur, could have been declared in an extra inner block:

```
|[ i: int
; |[ j: int; i:= 0; j:= N
  ; do  j ≠ i + 1 → ......... od
  ]| {R}
; present:= W(i)= X
]|
```

(5)   First we observe that W occurs only in the forms W(h) and W(i) in the statements of search; next we observe the two inequalities 0 < h < N and 0 ≤ i < N. Summing up we conclude that W(N) does *not* occur in the computation and that the characterization 'symbolic' is therefore entirely justified.   ■

The binary search is included in this collection of examples because it is an important, almost canonical, algorithm. It should be familiar in all its details to any educated computer scientist.

The longest upsequence

Consider the integer sequence $A(i: 0 \leq i < N)$ for $N \geq 1$. We shall denote the order of increasing subscript as 'the order from left to right'.

For any s that satisfies $0 \leq s \leq N$ we can form a 'subsequence of length s' by deleting an arbitrary $(N - s)$ number from the sequence s and maintaining the remaining s elements *in their original order*. An ascending subsequence of length s is called an **upsequence** of length s. (Note that all subsequences of length 1, as well as the empty subsequence, are upsequences.)

Find an algorithm to determine the maximal length of any upsequence contained in a sequence $A(i: 0 \leq i < N)$. (Note that this maximum length can be realized by more than one upsequence: for example, the sequence (3, 1, 1, 2, 5, 3) yields a maximal length of 4, realized by both (1, 1, 2, 5) and (1, 1, 2, 3).)

Let our postcondition be R, given by

> R: $k =$ the maximal length of any upsequence contained in
> $A(i: 0 \leq i < N)$

It is not difficult to satisfy ourselves that each element of the A sequence must be involved in the computation, and we (modestly) assume that this will be in order from left to right. In other words, we propose to introduce a second variable n and the invariant P1, given by

> P1: $1 \leq n \leq N \land$
> $k =$ the maximal length of any upsequence contained in
> $A(i: 0 \leq i < N)$

and a program of the structure

```
|[ n: int
; "establish P1 for  n = 1"
; do  n ≠ N →
```

```
        "increment n by 1 under invariance of P1"
    od
  ]|
```

Initialization is not a problem since the state $(n, k) = (1, 1)$ satisfies P1. The increment of $n := n + 1$, however, may require a modification of the value of k – the only other variable occurring in P1! Since the beginning of an upsequence is again an upsequence, the modification of k, if necessary, has the form $k := k + 1$, and "increment n by 1 under invariance of P1" therefore has the form:

```
    {P1 ∧ 1 ≦ n < N}
    if ... → k:= k + 1  ▯  ... → skip fi
  ; n:= n + 1 {P}
```

It only remains to determine the guards, that is, the conditions under which k must be incremented by 1 or left the same, respectively, so that it is guaranteed that, after the next increment of $n := n + 1$, P1 again holds.

Since A(n) is the next element that comes up for inspection, we can fill in the guards as follows:

```
    {P1 ∧ 1 ≦ n < N}
    if  m ≦ A(n) → k:= k + 1  ▯  A(n) < m → skip fi
  ; n:= n + 1
```

provided that the value of m is defined by

> **D:**   m = the minimal right-most element of any upsequence of
> length k contained in A(i: 0 ≦ i < n)

In other words, to keep P1 invariant, we need another variable m, besides k, which is a second derivative of A(i: 0 ≦ i < n).

Introducing m and choosing P1 ∧ D as invariant leads to

```
  |[ n, m: int
   ; k:= 1; n:= 1; m:= A(0)
   ; do n ≠ N →
                if m ≦ A(n)  →  k:= k + 1; m:= A(n)
                ▯ A(n) < m  →  ...
                fi; n:= n + 1
     od
  ]|
```

Observe that now n must be incremented by 1 under invariance of P1 ∧ D. In the first alternative the invariance of D is no problem: all upsequences of the new maximal length have A(n) as their right-most element, and this is then the new value of m.

But how are things in the second alternative, if $A(n) < m$? The new element $A(n)$ cannot then be used to form a longer upsequence, but perhaps it can be used to decrement the value of m. Instead of the last ... we have for the modification of m

```
{A(n) < m}
if m' ≤ A(n)  →  m:= A(n)
 ▯ A(n) < m'  →  skip
fi
```

provided that the value of m' is defined by

```
D':  m' = if k = 1  → "minus infinity"
          ▯ k > 1    the minimal right-most element of any
                     upsequence of length  k − 1  contained in
                     A(i: 0 ≤ i < n)
       fi
```

In other words, to keep D invariant we need m' as a next derivative of $A(i: 0 \le i < n)$. After introducing m' as a new variable and $P1 \wedge D \wedge D'$ as new invariant, we need an m'' for the invariance of D', etc. The conclusion is that we do not need a scalar m but an array m, given by P2, which replaces $D \wedge D' \wedge D'' \wedge \ldots$.

```
P2:   (A j: 1 ≤ j ≤ k:
                m(j) = the minimal right-most element of any
                       upsequence of length  j  contained in
                       A(i: 0 ≤ i < n) )
```

With invariant $P1 \wedge P2$, the macroscopic structure of our program is

```
|[ n: int
; m(i: 1 ≤ i < N + 1): array of int
; k:= 1; n:= 1; m:(1)= A(0) {P1 ∧ P2}
; do  n ≠ N → "increment n by 1 under invariance of
                 P1 ∧ P2"
    od
]|
```

From P2 it follows that $m(1)$ is the minimum of $A(i: 0 \le i < n)$, and furthermore that $m(j: 1 \le j \le k)$ is ascending. From this observation, how m must be modified if k remains constant follows (check this!); increment n by 1 under invariance of $P1 \wedge P2$ can be elaborated to

```
if m(k) ≤ A(n)  →  k:= k + 1; m:(k)= A(n)
▯  A(n) < m(1)  →  m:(1)= A(n)
▯  m(1) ≤ A(n)  ∧  A(n) < m(k)  →
    |[ j: int
    ; "determine  j  such that m(j − 1) ≤ A(n) < m(j)"
    ; m:(j)= A(n)
       ]|
fi; n:= n + 1
```

And, finally, for determine j such that $m(j − 1) ≤ A(n) < m(j)$ we appeal to the core of the binary search. More precisely, we maintain the invariant

$$1 ≤ i < j ≤ k ∧ m(i) ≤ A(n) < m(j)$$

The elaboration becomes

```
   {m(1) ≤ A(n) < m(k)  ∧  k ≥ 2}
|[ i: int; i:= 1; j:= k
; do  j − 1 ≠ i  →
           |[ h: int; h:= (i + j)div 2
           ; if m(h) ≤ A(n)  →  i:= h
             ▯  A(n) < m(h)  →  j:= h
             fi
             ]|
   od
]|
```

And with this the problem is solved with an $N \cdot \log N$ algorithm. Note that in the extreme cases ($k = 1$ or $k = N$) the computation time is proportional to N.

PART 1

0
General introduction

0.0 Predicate calculus

For a formal treatment of the concept of **predicate** we resort to a brief, informal introduction to logic. However, we shall go into the possibility of calculating with predicates extensively. To this end we shall treat a relatively large number of identities, indicating how, by their means, calculations can be performed.

A predicate is an expression which may be regarded as a Boolean function. The domains of the predicate and of the corresponding Boolean function are the same. In the greater part of our considerations the domain is the Cartesian product of a number of (infinite) sets named by their coordinates. The names of the coordinates may occur in the predicate. We shall often refer to these names as **variables**. As a rule the predicates we consider are total, that is, the corresponding Boolean functions are total functions. Only if they are partial, that is, not total, will this be mentioned explicitly.

Examples of (total) predicates on the (x, y) plane are:

$$x = y \qquad x^2 + y^2 \geqq 1 \qquad x \geqq 0$$

The assertion that a predicate is *true* in a point of the domain means that the corresponding Boolean function in that point has the value *true*. A predicate is *false* in a point of the domain if it is not *true* there.

Of course, we may also regard a predicate as a Boolean function of more variables than there are in the expression. As a result of this, two (constant) predicates are defined on any (non-empty) domain, namely:

- *true*, which is true in any point; and
- *false*, which is false in any point.

* \qquad * \qquad *

Now consider a fixed domain and a (large) collection of predicates on this domain. By means of the symbols

$\equiv$ equivalence,
$\wedge$ conjunction,
$\vee$ disjunction,
$\neg$ negation,
$\Rightarrow$ implication,

we construct new predicates from existing ones. The symbols $\equiv$, $\wedge$, $\vee$ and $\Rightarrow$ are used as binary infix operators, and the symbol $\neg$ as a unary prefix operator. Of the binary operators, $\equiv$, $\wedge$ and $\vee$ are both symmetric and associative, and $\Rightarrow$ is neither symmetric nor associative.

The relationship between a predicate thus composed and the composing predicates is, that for all predicates P, Q and R, we have:

- $P \equiv Q \equiv R$ is *true* in any point of the domain where an even number of the operands (here: P, Q and R) is *false*, and is *false* everywhere else;

- $P \wedge Q \wedge R$ is *true* in any point of the domain where each of the operands is *true*, and is *false* everywhere else;

- $P \vee Q \vee R$ is *false* in any point of the domain where each of the operands is *false*, and is *true* everywhere else;

- $\neg P$ is *true* in any point of the domain where P is *false*, and is *false* everywhere else;

- $P \Rightarrow Q$ is *false* in any point of the domain where P is *true* and Q is *false*, and is *true* everywhere else.

In order both to avoid ambiguities and to reduce the number of required brackets in formulae, a binding power is assigned to the operators: $\neg$ has the greatest binding power, then $\wedge$ and $\vee$, and finally $\equiv$ and $\Rightarrow$. This means that $\neg P \vee Q \equiv \neg P$ must be read as $((\neg P) \vee Q) \equiv \neg P$. This also means that $P \wedge Q \wedge R$ may not be written thus, because it is not clear which of the formulae $(P \wedge Q) \vee R$ or $P \wedge (Q \vee R)$ is meant.

*   *   *

In the collection of all predicates that we can now write, we are particularly interested in the subclass of the **valid** predicates. A predicate is valid if it is *true* in any point of the domain.

Before we go on to mention a whole series of valid predicates, we shall first give the rule which is of extreme importance for all calculations, namely the Substitution rule.

Substitution rule. If $P \equiv Q$ and a number of occurrences of P in the expression R are replaced by Q, then the (in)validity of R is not affected by this. ∎

A number of elementary, valid predicates are:

(0) $true$,

(1) $P \equiv P \equiv true$,

(2) $P \wedge P \equiv P$,

(3) $P \vee P \equiv P$,

(4) $P \wedge (Q \vee R) \equiv (P \wedge Q) \wedge (P \wedge R)$,

(5) $P \vee (Q \wedge R) \equiv (P \vee Q) \wedge (P \vee R)$,

(6) $P \wedge true \equiv P$,

(7) $P \vee true \equiv true$,

(8) $P \wedge false \equiv false$,

(9) $P \vee false \equiv P$.

If we analyse (1) as $P \equiv (P \equiv true)$, then according to the substitution rule we may, in any predicate in which $P \equiv true$ occurs, replace this combination by P, and vice versa, without affecting the (in)validity of R. We can express this property by saying that $true$ is the identity element of the operator $\equiv$. With this we can derive the validity of

(10) $P \equiv P$

from the validity of (1).

Furthermore, the validity of

(11) $P \wedge true$

follows from the validity of (7).

From (6) it appears that $true$ is the identity element of the disjunction. We usually express the validity of (2) and (3) by referring to the idempotency of the conjunction and the disjunction, respectively. We usually refer to (4) as the property that the conjunction distributes over the disjunction, and to (5) as the property that the disjunction distributes over the conjunction.

*   *   *

We shall now proceed to give a characterization of what we shall call a 'calculation'.

Suppose that on the basis of Consideration 0 we decide on the validity of $P \equiv Q$, and on the basis of Consideration 1 on the validity of $Q \equiv R$; then the validity of $P \equiv R$ follows by means of the Substitution rule (in two different ways).

For the sake of brevity, among other reasons, we denote this reasoning as the following 'calculation':

$$
\begin{array}{ll}
P & \\
= & \{\text{Consideration 0}\} \\
Q & \\
= & \{\text{Consideration 1}\} \\
R &
\end{array}
$$

The validity of $P \equiv R$ then follows from this, without mentioning the Substitution rule explicitly.

As an example we derive the validity of the second of the two absorption rules

(12) $P \wedge (P \vee Q) \; \equiv \; P$

(13) $P \vee (P \wedge Q) \; \equiv \; P$

from

$$
\begin{array}{ll}
P \vee (P \wedge Q) & \\
= & \{(6)\} \\
(P \vee true) \vee (P \wedge Q) & \\
= & \{(4)\} \\
P \wedge (true \vee Q) & \\
= & \{(7)\} \\
P \wedge true & \\
= & \{(6)\} \\
P &
\end{array}
$$

Note that at each step (Consideration) in the above calculation, we use the Substitution rule and the validity of (10). Since this will always be the case, we shall not refer to it again.

EXERCISE

E0   Show, by calculation, that $P \wedge (P \vee Q) \; \equiv \; P$ (12).

---

*   *   *

We continue our series of valid predicates:

(14) $false \equiv \neg true,$

(15) $P \wedge \neg P \equiv false,$

(16) $P \vee \neg P \equiv true,$

(17) $\neg \neg P \equiv P,$

(18) $\neg(P \wedge Q) \equiv \neg P \vee \neg Q,$

(19) $\neg(P \vee Q) \equiv \neg P \wedge \neg Q,$

(20) $\neg(P \equiv Q) \equiv \neg P \equiv Q.$

Rule (16) is known as the *tertium non datur*, the 'law' of excluded middle; rule (17) is the 'law' of double negation; rules (18) and (19) are the 'laws' of de Morgan. Rule (20) says that the brackets in this formula are irrelevant.

The two complement rules

(21) $P \wedge Q \equiv (P \vee \neg Q) \wedge Q$

(22) $P \vee Q \equiv (P \wedge \neg Q) \vee Q$

are of importance. They follow from the rules mentioned before in various ways. Rule (22), for example, follows from:

$$P \vee Q$$
$$= \quad \{(6)\}$$
$$(P \vee Q) \wedge true$$
$$= \quad \{(16)\}$$
$$(P \vee Q) \wedge (\neg Q \vee Q)$$
$$= \quad \{(5)\}$$
$$(P \wedge \neg Q) \vee Q$$

*   *   *

We continue our series of valid predicates with two rules which establish the relationship between $\equiv$, $\wedge$ and $\vee$:

(23) $(P \equiv Q) \vee R \equiv P \vee R \equiv Q \vee R$

(24) $P \wedge Q \equiv P \equiv Q \equiv P \vee Q$

Formula (23) states that the disjunction distributes over the equivalence. This is not true for the conjunction. For the conjunction it is true, though, that

(25) $(P \equiv Q) \vee \neg R \;\equiv\; P \wedge R \;\equiv\; Q \wedge R$

since

$$(P \equiv Q) \vee \neg R$$
$$= \quad \{(17)\}$$
$$\neg\neg(P \equiv Q) \vee \neg R$$
$$= \quad \{ \text{ twice } \quad (20)\}$$
$$(\neg P \equiv \neg Q) \vee \neg R$$
$$= \quad \{(23)\}$$
$$\neg P \vee \neg R \equiv \neg Q \vee \neg R$$
$$= \quad \{ \text{ twice } \quad (18)\}$$
$$\neg(P \wedge R) \equiv \neg(Q \wedge R)$$
$$= \quad \{ \text{ twice } \quad (20)\}$$
$$P \wedge R \equiv Q \wedge R$$

From (23) it follows that

(26) $\neg P \vee Q \;\equiv\; P \wedge Q \;\equiv\; Q$

and from (25) that

(27) $\neg P \vee Q \;\equiv\; P \wedge Q \;\equiv\; P$

EXERCISE

E1   Show that $\neg P \vee Q \equiv P \vee Q \equiv Q$, and $\neg P \vee Q \equiv P \vee Q \equiv P$ (27 and 28).

---

(24) follows from (26) and (27).

Next we prove the validity of

(28) $P \equiv Q \equiv (\neg P \vee Q) \wedge (\neg Q \vee P)$

$$P \equiv Q$$
$$= \quad \{(24)\}$$
$$P \wedge Q \;\equiv\; P \vee Q$$
$$= \quad \{(1)\}$$
$$P \wedge Q \;\equiv\; P \;\equiv\; P \;\equiv\; P \vee Q$$
$$= \quad \{(26)\}$$
$$P \wedge Q \;\equiv\; P \;\equiv\; \neg Q \vee P$$
$$= \quad \{(27)\}$$

$$\lnot P \lor Q \equiv \lnot Q \lor P$$
$$= \{(24), \text{ with } \lnot P \lor Q \text{ for } P \text{ and } \lnot Q \lor P \text{ for } Q\}$$
$$(\lnot P \lor Q) \land (\lnot Q \lor P) \equiv \lnot P \lor Q \lor \lnot Q \lor P$$
$$= \{(16), (7) \text{ and } (1)\}$$
$$(\lnot P \lor Q) \land (\lnot Q \lor P)$$

EXERCISES

E2   Show that $P \equiv Q \equiv (P \land Q) \lor (P \land Q)$.

E3   Show that $(P \lor Q) \land (P \lor R) \equiv (P \land Q) \lor (P \land R)$.

---

*   *   *

We conclude with the implication $\Rightarrow$. We have

(29) $(P \Rightarrow Q) \equiv P \land Q \equiv P$

from which, by means of (27), it follows that

(30) $(P \Rightarrow Q) \equiv \lnot P \lor Q$

and from this, with (26)

(31) $(P \Rightarrow Q) \equiv P \lor Q \equiv Q$

From (28) and (30) we deduce

(32) $P \equiv Q \equiv (P \Rightarrow Q) \land (Q \Rightarrow P)$

EXERCISE

E4   Show by calculation the validity of

$$(P \Rightarrow Q) \lor R \equiv (P \land R \Rightarrow Q \lor R)$$

and of

$$(P \Rightarrow Q) \lor \lnot R \equiv (P \land R \Rightarrow Q \land R).$$

In what follows, we shall regularly appeal to the validity of

(33) $false \implies P$

(34) $P \implies true$

(35) $P \wedge Q \implies P$

(36) $P \implies P \vee Q$

(37) $(true \implies P) \equiv P$

We say that P is stronger than Q or that Q is weaker than P if $P \implies Q$ holds.

According to (33) *false* is stronger than any predicate, and because of (34) any predicate is stronger than *true*.

According to (35) a conjunction can be weakened by leaving out a conjunct, and because of (36) a disjunction can be strengthened by leaving out a disjunct.

*   *   *

If $P \implies Q$ and $Q \implies R$ hold, then $P \implies R$ also holds, because

$$P$$
$$= \quad \{P \implies Q \text{ holds, and therefore also } P \equiv P \wedge Q\}$$
$$P \wedge Q$$
$$= \quad \{Q \implies R \text{ holds, and therefore also } Q \equiv Q \wedge R\}$$
$$P \wedge Q \wedge R$$
$$= \quad P \implies Q \text{ holds, and therefore also } P \wedge Q \equiv P$$
$$P \wedge R$$

so that $P \equiv P \wedge R$ holds, and therefore also $P \implies R$.

For the sake of brevity, among other things, we can sum up the above reasoning in a calculation:

$$P$$
$$\Rightarrow \quad \{\text{argument why } P \implies Q \text{ holds}\}$$
$$Q$$
$$\Rightarrow \quad \{\text{argument why } Q \implies R \text{ holds}\}$$
$$R$$

with the conclusion that $P \implies R$ holds.

The following illustrates this:

(38) $(P \implies Q) \implies (P \vee R \implies Q \vee R)$

$$(P \Rightarrow Q$$
$$\Rightarrow \quad \{(36), \text{ with } P \Rightarrow Q \text{ for } P \text{ and } R \text{ for } Q\}$$
$$(P \Rightarrow Q) \lor R$$
$$= \quad \{\text{Exercise E4}\}$$
$$P \lor R \Rightarrow Q \lor R$$

*   *   *

The reader is not expected to learn all the formulae by heart, but should learn how to handle them. The following exercises may be helpful in this.

Only after (really after) the reader has become sufficiently familiar with formulae of the above kind can references to them be disposed of in calculations (in braces) by the statement 'elementary'.

EXERCISES

E5 Show that:

(i) the validity of Q follows from the validity of P and of $P \Rightarrow Q$,

(ii) the validity of P follows from the validity of $P \land Q$,

(iii) the validity of Q follows from the validity of P and of $P \Rightarrow Q$.

E6 Show by calculation that:

(i) $P \land Q \quad \equiv \text{ false } \equiv \neg P \lor \neg Q,$

(ii) $P \land Q \quad \equiv \neg P \land \neg Q \equiv P \equiv \neg Q,$

(iii) $P \land R \quad \equiv Q \land R \equiv \neg P \land R \equiv \neg Q \land R,$

(iv) $P \lor R \quad \equiv Q \lor R \equiv \neg P \lor R \equiv \neg Q \lor R.$

E7 Show by calculation that:

(i) $(\neg P \lor Q) \land (\neg Q \lor R) \land P \land \neg R \equiv \text{false},$

(ii) $(P \land Q) \lor (R \land S) \lor \neg P \lor \neg R \lor \neg(Q \lor S),$

(iii) $\neg P \lor Q \lor ((P \lor Q) \land (\neg P \lor \neg Q)),$

(iv) $(P \land Q) \lor (Q \land R) \lor (R \land P) \equiv (P \lor Q) \land (Q \lor R) \land (R \lor P).$

E8 Show by calculation that:

(i) $(P \equiv Q) \Rightarrow (P \Rightarrow Q),$

(ii) $(P \Rightarrow Q) \Rightarrow (P \land R \Rightarrow Q \land R),$

(iii) $R \land (P \Rightarrow Q) \equiv (\neg R \lor P \Rightarrow R \land Q)$

(iv) $(P \land Q \Rightarrow R) \equiv (P \Rightarrow \neg Q \lor R).$

*   *   *

A completely different way to make new predicates from existing ones is by means of **universal quantification** and **existential quantification**.

If P and Q are predicates, then so are the expressions

$$(\underline{A} \; x: P: Q)$$

and

$$(\underline{E} \; x: P: Q)$$

The symbol $\underline{A}$ (sometimes given the special symbol $\forall$) is the universal quantifier, and the symbol $\underline{E}$ (or $\exists$) the existential quantifier. The name x is the **dummy**, P the **domain** and Q the **term** of the quantification.

It holds that:

(39) $\neg(\underline{A} \; x: P: Q) \;\equiv\; (\underline{E} \; x: P: \neg Q)$
(40) $\neg(\underline{E} \; x: P: Q) \;\equiv\; (\underline{A} \; x: P: \neg Q)$

These rules are known as the (generalized) laws of de Morgan.

As a result of these laws all formulae about quantification come in pairs, and we shall therefore present them in pairs.

It holds that:

(41a) $(\underline{A} \; x: false: P)$
(41b) $\neg(\underline{E} \; x: false: P)$
(42a) $(\underline{A} \; x: P \wedge Q: R) \;\equiv\; (\underline{A} \; x: P: \neg Q \vee R)$
(42b) $(\underline{E} \; x: P \vee Q: R) \;\equiv\; (\underline{E} \; x: P: Q \wedge R)$
(43a) $(\underline{A} \; x: P: Q) \;\Rightarrow\; (\underline{A} \; x: P: Q \vee R)$
(43b) $(\underline{E} \; x: P: Q) \;\Rightarrow\; (\underline{E} \; x: P: Q \vee R)$

Rules (41a) and (41b) state that the universal quantification over an empty domain is *true*, and that existential quantification over an empty domain is *false*.

Rules (42a) and (42b) indicate how a domain and a term of quantification can change places.

Rules (43a) and (43b) provide the possibility of weakening a quantification by weakening the term.

The first of the rules

(44a) $(\underline{A} \; x: P: true)$
(44b) $\neg(\underline{E} \; x: P: false)$

follows from:

$(\underline{A} \ x: P: true)$
= $\{true \ \equiv \ true \ \vee \ true, \ \ (43a)\}$
$(\underline{A}\ \underline{x}: P \wedge \neg true: true)$
= $\{P \wedge \neg true \ \equiv \ false\}$
$(\underline{A} \ x: false: true)$
= $\{(41a)\}$
    $true$

EXERCISES

E9   Show that:

$$(\underline{A} \ x: P: Q) \ \equiv \ (\underline{A} \ x: P: P \wedge Q)$$

and

$$(\underline{E} \ x: P: Q) \ \equiv \ (\underline{E} \ x: P: \neg P \vee Q)$$

E10   Show by calculation that:

    (i) $(\underline{A} \ x: P \wedge Q: P)$,
    (ii) $(\underline{A} \ x: P: P \vee Q)$,
    (iii)   the validity of $(\underline{A} \ x: P: Q)$ follows from the validity of $P \Rightarrow Q$,
    (iv) $(\underline{E} \ x: P: \neg P) \ \equiv \ false$,
    (v) $(\underline{E} \ x: P: Q \wedge R) \ \Rightarrow \ (\underline{E} \ x: P: Q)$,
    (vi) $(\underline{E} \ x: P: Q \wedge R) \ \Rightarrow \ (\underline{E} \ x: P: Q) \ \wedge \ (\underline{E} \ x: P: R)$,
   (vii) $(\underline{A} \ x: P: Q) \ \vee \ (\underline{A} \ x: P: R) \ \Rightarrow \ (\underline{A} \ x: P: Q \vee R)$,
  (viii) $(\underline{A} \ x: P: \neg Q) \ \equiv \ (\underline{A} \ x: Q: \neg P)$
    (ix) $(\underline{E} \ x: P: Q) \ \equiv \ (\underline{E} \ x: Q: P)$.

E11   Show that it is impossible to reduce a universally quantified expression to *false* with the rules given so far.

---

        *   *   *

Before we give the most important of the remaining calculation rules, we shall discuss some notational matters.

- If R is an expression, x a variable, and E an expression of a type corresponding to x, then R_E^x is the expression obtained from R by replacing any occurrence of x in R by E. Thus we have, for example:

$$(x + y)_{x-y}^x = x - y + y \quad \text{and} \quad R_x^x \equiv R \quad \text{and}$$
$$(x = E)_E^x \equiv (E = E_E^x) \quad \text{and} \quad (P_y^x)_x^y \equiv P_x^y$$

- If R is a quantified expression, then it holds (by definition) that the name of the dummy does not occur in R. We can avoid this by agreeing that we shall choose a brand new name for the dummy when introducing a quantified expression, i.e. a name that has not so far occurred anywhere else. Thus we have, for example, for any completely new y

(45a) $(\underline{A}\ x:\ P:\ Q)\ \equiv\ (\underline{A}\ y:\ P^x_y:\ Q^x_y)$
(45b) $(\underline{E}\ x:\ P:\ Q)\ \equiv\ (\underline{E}\ y:\ P^x_y:\ Q^x_y)$

known as the rules for 'renaming the dummy'.

One of the reasons why we always put quantified expressions in brackets is to underline the fact that with the opening bracket the current collection of names is extended with a name, i.e. with that of the dummy, and that at the corresponding closing bracket this name disappears from the collection again.

We shall not go into the matter of the (textual) scope of names at present. At a later stage we shall return to it, when the structure of programs comes up for discussion.

$$*\qquad*\qquad*$$

For any R in which x does not occur, we have

(46a) $(\underline{A}\ x:\ P:\ Q)\ \vee\ R\ \equiv\ (\underline{A}\ x:\ P:\ Q\ \vee\ R)$
(46b) $(\underline{E}\ x:\ P:\ Q)\ \wedge\ R\ \equiv\ (\underline{E}\ x:\ P:\ Q\ \wedge\ R)$

and for any non-empty domain, i.e. for a domain P for which $(\underline{E}\ x:\ P:\ true)$ holds,

(47a) $(\underline{A}\ x:\ P:\ Q)\ \wedge\ R\ \equiv\ (\underline{A}\ x:\ P:\ Q\ \wedge\ R)$
(47b) $(\underline{E}\ x:\ P:\ Q)\ \vee\ R\ \equiv\ (\underline{E}\ x:\ P:\ Q\ \vee\ R)$

Rules (46) and (47) are rules for distribution of conjunction and disjunction over universal and existential quantifications. Note that (47) is not permitted in an empty domain.

The validity of the second of the Substitution rules is illustrated as follows:

(48a) $(\underline{A}\ y:\ x = y:\ R)\ \equiv\ R^y_x$
(48b) $(\underline{E}\ y:\ x = y:\ R)\ \equiv\ R^y_x$

$$\begin{aligned}
&(\underline{E}\ y:\ x = y:\ R)\\
=\ &\quad \{(x = y)\ \equiv\ (x = y)\ \wedge\ (x = y),\ (42b)\}
\end{aligned}$$

$$(\underline{E} \; y: x = y: x = y \wedge R)$$
$$= \quad \{x = y \;\; \wedge \;\; R \;\; \equiv \;\; x = y \;\; \wedge \;\; R_x^y\}$$
$$(\underline{E} \; y: x = y: x = y \;\; \wedge \;\; R_x^y)$$
$$= \quad \{(42b)\}$$
$$(\underline{E} \; y: x = y: R_x^y)$$
$$= \quad \{y \text{ does not occur in } R_x^y; \; R_x^y \;\; \equiv \;\; \textit{false} \vee R_x^y; \;\; (47b)\}$$
$$(\underline{E} \; y: x = y: \textit{false}) \;\; \vee \;\; R_x^y$$
$$= \quad \{\text{with}(44b)\}$$
$$R_x^y$$

With E being an expression in which y does not occur, a somewhat more general formulation of the Substitution rules is given by:

(49a) $(\underline{A} \; y: y = E: P) \;\; \equiv \;\; P_E^y$

(49b) $(\underline{E} \; y: y = E: P) \;\; \equiv \;\; P_E^y$

EXERCISE

E12   Check how (48) follows from (49).

Note that by means of (48) and (49) we are able to reduce a universal quantification to *false* and an existential quantification to *true*, ingredients that were previously missing (compare with Exercise E11). Together with the possibility of splitting domains, as given by (50), this completes our calculus.

(50a) $(\underline{A} \; x: P \vee Q: R) \;\; \equiv \;\; (\underline{A} \; x: P: R) \;\; \wedge \;\; (\underline{A} \; x: Q: R)$

(50b) $(\underline{E} \; x: P \vee Q: R) \;\; \equiv \;\; (\underline{E} \; x: P: R) \;\; \vee \;\; (\underline{E} \; x: Q: R)$

*   *   *

To conclude, we give a number of examples.

EXAMPLE 1

$(\underline{E} \; x: P: P)$ holds for a non-empty domain, as

$$(\underline{E} \; x: P: P)$$
$$= \quad \{\text{elementary}\}$$
$$(\underline{E} \; x: P: P \wedge \textit{true})$$

$=$ $\{P \wedge P \equiv P$ and (42b)$\}$
    $(\underline{\text{E}}\ x\colon P\colon true)$
$=$ $\{P$ is not empty$\}$
    $true$

EXAMPLE 2

It holds that $(\underline{\text{A}}\ x\colon P\colon Q)\ \wedge\ (\underline{\text{A}}\ x\colon P\colon R)\ \equiv\ (\underline{\text{A}}\ x\colon P\colon Q \wedge R)$, as

        $(\underline{\text{A}}\ x\colon P\colon Q)\ \wedge\ (\underline{\text{A}}\ x\colon P\colon R)$
$=$ $\{$with (42a) or with Exercise E10 (viii)$\}$
        $(\underline{\text{A}}\ x\colon \neg Q\colon \neg P)\ \wedge\ (\underline{\text{A}}\ x\colon \neg R\colon \neg P)$
$=$ $\{(50a)\}$
        $(\underline{\text{A}}\ x\colon \neg Q \vee \neg R\colon \neg P)$
$=$ $\{$with (42a)$\}$
        $(\underline{\text{A}}\ x\colon P\colon Q \wedge R)$

EXAMPLE 3

With x and y from the integers, it holds that

$$(\underline{\text{A}}\ x\colon x = 2 \cdot y \wedge y > 0\colon 4 \mid x)\ \equiv\ (y \leq 0 \vee 2 \mid y)$$

as:

        $(\underline{\text{A}}\ x\colon x = 2 \cdot y \vee y > 0\colon 4 \mid x)$
$=$ $\{(42a)\}$
        $(\underline{\text{A}}\ x\colon x = 2 \cdot y\colon y \leq 0 \vee 4 \mid x)$
$=$ $\{(49a)\}$
        $(y \leq 0 \vee 4 \mid x)^{x}_{2 \cdot y}$
$=$ $\{$arithmetic$\}$
        $y \leq 0 \vee 2 \mid y$

EXERCISES

E13   Show by calculation that, for a non-empty domain P, it holds that:

    (i) $\neg(\underline{\text{A}}\ x\colon P\colon \neg P)$,

    (ii) $(\underline{\text{E}}\ x\colon P\colon P)$,

    (iii) $(\underline{\text{A}}\ x\colon P\colon Q)\ \Rightarrow\ (\underline{\text{E}}\ x\colon P\colon Q)$.

E14   Show that:

(i) $(\underline{E}\ x: P: Q)\ \vee\ (\underline{E}\ x: P: R)\ \equiv\ (\underline{E}\ x: P: Q \vee R)$,

(ii) $(\underline{A}\ x: P: Q \vee R)\ \Rightarrow\ (\underline{E}\ x: P: Q)\ \vee\ (\underline{A}\ x: P: R)$.

E15   Let $P(i: i \geq 0)$ be a sequence of predicates. Show that for any natural number n (i.e. $n \geq 0$) it holds that:

(i) $(\underline{A}\ i: 0 \leq i < n: P(i))$ for $n = 0$, and
$(\underline{A}\ i: 0 \leq i < n + 1: P(i))\ \equiv\ (\underline{A}\ i: 0 \leq i < n: P(i))\ \wedge\ P(n)$;

(ii) $\neg(\underline{E}\ i: 0 \leq i < n: P(i))$ for $n = 0$, and
$(\underline{E}\ i: 0 \leq i < n + 1: P(i))\ \equiv\ (\underline{E}\ i: 0 \leq i < n: P(i))\ \vee\ P(n)$.

E16   Show that for any sequence $X(i: 0 \leq i < N)$ of integers it holds that:

$$(\underline{A}\ i: 0 \leq i < N: (\underline{A}\ j: 0 \leq j < N: X(i) \cdot X(j) \geq 0))\ \equiv$$
$$(\underline{A}\ i: 0 \leq i < N: X(i) \geq 0) \vee (\underline{A}\ j: 0 \leq j < N: X(j) \geq 0)$$

0.1   Mathematical induction

In what follows, 'numbers' should be taken to mean integers, and 'natural numbers' to mean numbers that are at least 0.

For $P(i: i \geq 0)$, a sequence of predicates, we denote the ith element by $P(i)$ or by Pi.

'Mathematical induction' refers to a specific method to prove expressions of the form $(\underline{A}\ n: n \geq 0: Pn)$. Instead of proving Pn for arbitrary natural n, it suffices to demonstrate the weaker expression $Pn\ \vee\ (\underline{E}\ i: 0 \leq i < n: \neg Pi)$.

More precisely, it holds that

(0) $(\underline{A}\ n: n \geq 0: Pn)$

$\equiv$

$(\underline{A}\ n: n \geq 0: Pn\ \vee\ (\underline{E}\ i: 0 \leq i < n: \neg Pi))$

known as 'the postulate of mathematical induction'.

It must be emphasized that (for the time being) it is essential that the domain of universal quantification is that of natural numbers.

The most common formulation of the postulate of mathematical induction is:

(1) $(\underline{A}\ n: n \geq 0: Pn)$

$\equiv$

$P0\ \wedge\ (\underline{A}\ n: n \geq 1: Pn \vee \neg P(n - 1))$

(The proof of $P0$ is usually called 'the basis of the induction', and the proof of $Pn \ \lor \ \neg P(n - 1)$ usually 'the step of the induction'.)

Both induction principles are (fortunately) the same. In general, formulation (0) is preferred to (1), because the expression $Pn \ \lor \ (\underline{E}\ i: 0 \le i < n: \neg Pi)$ for $n \ge 1$ is weaker than the expression $Pn \ \lor \ \neg P(n - 1)$, and therefore at least as easily proved.

EXERCISES

E0   Show that the validity of (1) follows from that of (0).

E1   Show that any natural number of at least 2 is the product of primes.

The decision to prove $(\underline{A}\ n: n \ge 0: Pn)$ by mathematical induction is idempotent, i.e. if we define for $n \ge 0$

Qn: $Pn \ \lor \ (\underline{E}\ i: 0 \le i < n: \neg Pi)$
Rn: $Qn \ \lor \ (\underline{E}\ i: 0 \le i < n: \neg Qi)$

then $(\underline{A}\ n: n \ge 0: Qn \equiv Rn)$ follows, so that the decision to prove $(\underline{A}\ n: n \ge 0: Qn)$ by mathematical induction is an empty decision.

PROOF

For any $n \ge 0$ it holds that:

$\quad Rn$
$=\quad$ {definition Rn}
$\quad Qn \ \lor \ (\underline{E}\ i: 0 \le i < n: \neg Qi)$
$=\quad$ {definition Qn}
$\quad Pn \ \lor \ (\underline{E}\ i: 0 \le i < n: \neg Pi) \lor (\underline{E}\ i: 0 \le i < n: \neg Qi)$
$=\quad$ {predicate calculus (compare Exercise E14 in Section 0.0)}
$\quad Pn \ \lor \ (\underline{E}\ i: 0 \le i < n: \neg Pi \lor \neg Qi)$
$=\quad$ {because of the Remark below}
$\quad Pn \ \lor \ (\underline{E}\ i: 0 \le i < n: \neg Pi)$
$=\quad$ {definition Qn}
$\quad Qn$

Remark. For any $i \geq 0$ it holds that:

$$\begin{aligned}
& true \\
= \quad & \{\text{definition } Qi\} \\
& (Pi \;\Rightarrow\; Qi) \\
= \quad & \{\text{predicate calculus}\} \\
& (Pi \wedge Qi \;\equiv\; Pi) \\
= \quad & \{\text{predicate calculus}\} \\
& (\neg Pi \vee \neg Qi \;\equiv\; \neg Pi)
\end{aligned}$$

∎

EXERCISE

E2   For any subset S of the natural numbers it holds that

$(\underline{E} \; x: x \geq 0: x \text{ in } S)$

$\equiv$

$(\underline{E} \; x: x \geq 0: x \text{ in } S \;\wedge\; (\underline{A} \; y: 0 \leq y < x: \neg(y \text{ in } S)))$

put in classical terms as 'any non-empty subset of the natural numbers has a smallest element'.

Show that this postulate is the same as the postulate of mathematical induction.

0.2   Remaining concepts

This section discusses a number of concepts frequently used in programming which, in their notation or use, deviate from what is common.

0.2.0   *General*

The following symbols are used:

$=$	pronounced	'equals'
$\neq$		'does not equal'
$\geq$		'at least'
$\leq$		'at most'
$>$		'larger than'
$<$		'smaller than'

The natural numbers are the (integer) numbers which are at least 0. If x is from a domain of N, $N \geq 0$, consecutive numbers which start at k, we usually write this as $k \leq x < k + N$.

The empty trajectory of natural numbers, which starts at 0, can thus be characterized by natural numbers only: $0 \leq x < 0$.

By the notation $f(x: P)$ we understand that f is a function of one argument, and that it is defined on the domain P.

The integer function $f(x: p \leq x < q)$, where $p \leq q$, may be described as:

- ascending, i.e. means $(\underline{A}\ x: p + 1 \leq x < q: f(x - 1) \leq f(x))$;
- descending, i.e. $(\underline{A}\ x: p + 1 \leq x < q: f(x - 1) \geq f(x))$;
- increasing, i.e. $(\underline{A}\ x: p + 1 \leq x < q: f(x - 1) < f(x))$;
- decreasing, i.e. $(\underline{A}\ x: p + 1 \leq x < q: f(x - 1) > f(x))$;
- monotone, i.e. ascending or descending;
- constant, i.e. ascending and descending.

A function $f(x: p \leq x < q)$ is very often called a finite sequence of length $q - p$.

Two sequences $f(x: p \leq x < q)$ and $g(x: p \leq x < q)$, with $p \leq q$, are equal (notation: $f = g$) means

$$(\underline{A}\ x: p \leq x < q: f(x) = g(x))$$

For two sequences $f(x: p \leq x < q)$ and $g(x: p \leq x < q)$, with $p \leq q$, 'f is lexicographically smaller than g' (notation: $f < g$) means

$$(\underline{E}\ x: p \leq x < q: f(x) < g(x) \quad \wedge \quad (\underline{A}\ y: p \leq y < x: f(y) = g(y)))$$

The lexicographic ordering is a total ordering, i.e. for any pair of sequences f and g, with the same domain, we have

$$f < g \quad \vee \quad f = g \quad \vee \quad g < f$$

We write the maximum of two numbers x and y as x **max** y, and the minimum as x **min** y.

For all x, y and z it holds that:

$$(z = x\ \textbf{max}\ y) \equiv (z = x \vee z = y) \quad \wedge \quad z \geq x \quad \wedge \quad z \geq y$$
$$(z = x\ \textbf{min}\ y) \equiv (Z = x \vee z = y) \quad \wedge \quad z \leq x \quad \wedge \quad z \leq y$$

The operators **max** and **min** are symmetric, associative and idempotent. The identity element of **max** is $-inf$; the identity element of **min** is $+inf$.

Sometimes we want to regard a predicate P as an equation in the unknown x. Then we write this as $x: P$. Thus the equation $z: z = x\ \textbf{max}\ y$ has exactly one solution for any x and y.

The equation $x: z = x$ **max** y has no solution for $y > z$, and exactly one solution for $y < z$.

The weakest solution of $X: X \Rightarrow P$ is P.

0.2.1 Other quantified expressions

If P is a predicate, E an expression of the type integer, and if the equation

$$x: (P \wedge E \neq 0)$$

has a finite number of solutions, then

$$(\underline{S}\ x: P: E)$$

is also an expression of the type integer. The symbol $\underline{S}$ (sometimes written Σ) is the summator (summation quantifier); x is the dummy of the quantified expression, P the domain and E the term.

We give a number of calculation rules. It holds that:

(0) $(\underline{S}\ x: \mathit{false}: E) = 0$

(1) $(\underline{S}\ x: x = y: E) = E_y^x$

(2) $(\underline{S}\ x: P: E) + (\underline{S}\ x: Q: E) = (\underline{S}\ x: P \vee Q: E) + (\underline{S}\ x: P \wedge Q: E)$

(3) $(\underline{S}\ x: P: E0) + (\underline{S}\ x: P: E1) = (\underline{S}\ x: P: E0 + E1)$

(4) $E0 \cdot (\underline{S}\ x: P: E1) = (\underline{S}\ x: P: E0 \cdot E1)$ provided that x does not occur in $E0$

(5) For a fresh y, $(\underline{S}\ x: P: E) = (\underline{S}\ y: P_y^x: E_y^x)$

The rules speak for themselves.

We usually satisfy the requirement that the number of solutions of $x: (P \wedge E \neq 0)$ is finite by choosing the domain P of the summation as finite.

*   *   *

Provided that it is finite, the number of solutions of $x: P \wedge Q$ is by definition equal to the 'numerically quantified expression'

$$(\underline{N}\ x: P: Q)$$

The symbol $\underline{N}$ is the 'numerical quantifier' (the N is from 'the number of').

It holds that

(6) $(\underline{N}\ x:\ P:\ Q) = (\underline{N}\ x:\ P \wedge Q:\ true)$

For the rest the calculation rules follow from the one for the summation, since it holds by definition that

(7) $(\underline{N}\ x:\ P:\ true) = (\underline{S}\ x:\ P:\ 1)$

Universal and existential quantification can be formulated for finite domains in terms of numerical quantification:

(8) $(\underline{A}\ x:\ P:\ Q) \equiv ((\underline{N}\ x:\ P:\ \neg Q) = 0)$
(9) $(\underline{E}\ x:\ P:\ Q) \equiv ((\underline{N}\ x:\ P:\ Q) \geq 1)$

The validity of de Morgan's laws would then follow from the validity of

$$((\underline{N}\ x:\ P:\ Q) = 0) \equiv ((\underline{N}\ x:\ P:\ Q) < 1)$$

– a genuine triviality.

*   *   *

If the integer function $f(x)$ is defined on a finite domain P, we write the maximum of f on P as

$(\mathbf{MAX}\ x:\ P:\ f(x))$

and the minimum as

$(\mathbf{MIN}\ x:\ P:\ f(x))$

It holds that:

(10) $(\mathbf{MAX}\ x:\ false:\ f(x)) = -inf$
(11) $(\mathbf{MAX}\ x:\ x = E:\ f(x)) = f(E)$, provided that x does not occur in E
(12) $(\mathbf{MAX}\ x:\ P \vee Q:\ f(x))$
          $= (\mathbf{MAX}\ x:\ P:\ f(x))\ \mathbf{max}\ (\mathbf{MAX}\ x:\ Q:\ f(x))$
(13)   for a non-empty domain
$$E + (\mathbf{MAX}\ x:\ P:\ f(x)) = (\mathbf{MAX}\ x:\ P:\ E + f(x)),$$
          provided that x does not occur in E.

The connection between **MIN** and **MAX** is given by:

(14)   (**MIN** x: P: $f(x)$ + (**MAX** x: P: $f(x)$)) = 0

and from this similar rules then follow for **MIN**.

We mention another definition of **MAX**:

(15) z = (**MAX** x: P: $f(x)$))
$\equiv$ ($\underline{E}$ y: P: $z = f(y)$) $\wedge$ ($\underline{A}$ x: P: $f(x) \leqq z$)
valid for a non-empty domain.

0.3 Miscellaneous exercises

E0   Given a number N, $N \geqq 1$, and a sequence $X(i: 0 \leqq i < N)$ of integers, represent the following assertions in formulae:

(a)   All values of the sequence are positive.

(b)   The number p occurs as often in $X(i: 0 \leqq i < j)$ as it does in $X(i: j \leqq i < N)$.

(c)   The number r equals the maximal length of some consecutive subsequence of $X(i: 0 \leqq i < N)$, of which all elements have the same value.

(d)   The sequence does not contain two equal values.

(e)   The sequence is a permutation of the numbers 0 up to and including $N - 1$.

(f)   The sequence $r(i: 0 \leqq i < N)$ contains the elements of $X(i: 0 \leqq i < N)$ in increasing order.

(g)   The number k is the smallest index for which $X(k) = w$.

(h) r is the sum of the positive numbers of the sequence.

(i) y is the number of index pairs (i, j) for which the sum starting from and including $X(0)$ up to and including $X(i)$ equals the sum starting from and including $X(j)$ up to and excluding $X(N)$.

(j) r is the number of times that the maximum of the sequence is included in the sequence.

E1   Determine the weakest solution for each of the equations:

(a) X: $X \Rightarrow P$,

(b) X: $X \wedge P \Rightarrow Q$,

(c) X: $X \vee (P \wedge Q) \Rightarrow Q$,

(d) X: $X \vee Q \Rightarrow P \vee Q$,

(e) X: $P \Rightarrow P \vee Q$.

E2   Determine the strongest solution for each of the equations:

(a) X: $X \Rightarrow P$,

(b) X: $P \Rightarrow X$,

(c) X: $P \Rightarrow X \vee Q$.

E3   Characterize the solutions of:

(a) X: $P \wedge X \equiv Q$,

(b) X: $(P \vee \neg Q) \wedge X \equiv P \equiv Q$.

E4   Give a recurrent definition of $(\underline{S}\ x: 0 \leq x < N: f(x))$ for a given sequence of numbers $f(x: 0 \leq x < N)$, and also of $(\textbf{MAX}\ x: 0 \leq x < N: f(x))$.

E5   Give a recurrent definition for lexicographic ordering.

E6   Prove by formal manipulation (using the definition for lexicographic ordering) that for any pair of sequences f and g with the same domain:

$$\neg(f < g)\ \wedge\ \neg(g < f)\ \equiv\ (f = g)$$

E7   Show by means of predicate calculus that for any sequence $P(i: i \geq 0)$ of predicates:

$$(\underline{A}\ i: i \geq 0: P(i))\ \equiv\ (\underline{A}\ i: i \geq 0: (\underline{A}\ j: 0 \leq j \leq i: P(j)))$$

E8   In terms of the predicate sequence $P(i: i \geq 0)$ we define the predicate sequence $Q(j: j \geq 0)$, in terms of which we define the predicate sequence $R(k: k \geq 0)$:

$Q(0) \equiv P(0)$ $Q(j + 1) \equiv Q(j) \vee P(j + 1)$ for all $j: j \geq 0$
$R(0) \equiv Q(0)$ $R(k + 1) \equiv R(k) \vee Q(k + 1)$ for all $k: k \geq 0$

Prove or refute:

$$(\underline{A}\ n: n \geq 0: Q(n)\ \equiv\ P(n))$$
$$(\underline{A}\ n: n \geq 0: R(n)\ \equiv\ Q(n))$$

E9   Prove by means of the definitions of **max** and **min**:

(a) $x + y \geq x\ \textbf{max}\ y\ \equiv\ x \geq 0\ \wedge\ y \geq 0$,

(b) $x + (y\ \textbf{max}\ z)\ =\ (x + y)\ \textbf{max}\ (x + z)$,

(c) $(x\ \textbf{max}\ y = x\ \textbf{min}\ y)\ \equiv\ (x = y)$.

E10   Show that for any sequence of numbers $X(i: 0 \leq i < N)$, $N \geq 1$, and for any integer M:

$$(\underline{S}\ i: 0 \leq i < N: X(i)) < M\ \ \vee\ \ (\underline{E}\ i: 0 \leq i < N: N \cdot X(i) \geq M)$$

– the 'Pigeon hole principle'.

E11   Given N numbers, $N \geq 3$, show that among these N numbers there are at least two whose sum or difference is a multiple of N.

E12   The sequence $F(i: i \geq 0)$ of Fibonacci numbers is defined by the recurrence scheme

$$F(0) = 0; \ F(1) = 1;$$

for all $n: n \geq 0: F(n + 2) = F(n + 1) + F(n)$.
   Prove that for all $n: n \geq 0$:

$$F(2 \cdot n + 1) = (F(n))^2 + (F(n + 1))^2$$
$$F(2 \cdot n + 2) = 2 \cdot F(n) \cdot F(n + 1) + (F(n + 1))^2$$

E13   For a sequence $X(i: 0 \leq i < N)$ we define s by:

$$s = (\mathbf{MIN} \ p: 0 \leq p < N \ \wedge \ (\underline{A} \ q: p \leq q < N: X(p) \leq X(q)): p)$$

Prove that $(\underline{A} \ r: 0 \leq r < s: X(r) > X(s))$.

E14   Prove that for any sequence of numbers $X(i: 0 \leq i < N)$, $N \geq 1$:

$$(\underline{A} \ i: 1 \leq i < N: X(0) < X(i))$$
$$\equiv (\underline{A} \ i: 1 \leq i < N: (\underline{E} \ j: 0 \leq j < i: X(j) < X(i)))$$

E15   Prove that for any sequence of numbers $X(i: 0 \leq i < N)$, $N \geq 1$, and for any number M:

$$(\underline{E} \ i: 0 \leq i < N: X(i) \geq M) \equiv ((\mathbf{MAX} \ i: 0 \leq i < N: X(i)) \geq M)$$

and

$$(\underline{A} \ i: 0 \leq i < N: X(i) \geq M) \equiv ((\mathbf{MIN} \ i: 0 \leq i < N: X(i)) \geq M)$$

1
Functional specifications and proof obligations

So far the text of this appendix has been more or less self-contained; from now on this will no longer be the case, because the text will refer to the lecture notes in Part 0. It is assumed that the reader is acquainted with the relevant material.

Before embarking on the exercises the most important concepts will be summarized. For the sake of simplicity we choose the integers as the domain of local variables.

For a statement list S and for predicates P and Q the validity of the expression

$|[$ x: int $\{P\}$; S $\{Q\}$ $]|$

means that, for an initial state which satisfies the precondition P, execution of S effects a final state which satisfies the postcondition of Q.

This indicates a relation between expressions of the form $|]$ x: int $\{P\}$; S $\{Q\}$ $]|$ and an appreciation of this expression as a machine-performable code. This mechanistic interpretation will play hardly any part in what is to follow.

In many programming problems, P and Q are given, and $|[$ x: int $\{P\}$; S $\{Q\}$ $]|$ can be regarded as an equation in S: for some S it is a valid expression and for some (most) S it is not. Therefore such a problem can be briefly summed up as:

S: $|[$ x: int $\{P\}$; S $\{Q\}$ $]|$

*   *   *

For arbitrary predicates P and Q, statement lists S, S0 and S1, Boolean expressions B0 and B1, and arbitrary integer expression E, it holds by definition that:

147

(0) $|[$ x: int $\{P\}$; skip $\{Q\}$ $]|$ means

$$P \Rightarrow Q$$

– the 'postulate of skip'.

(1) $|[$ x, y: int $\{P\}$; x:= E $\{Q\}$ $]|$ means

$$P \Rightarrow Q_E^x$$

– the 'postulate of the assignment'.

(2) $|[$ x: int $\{P\}$; S0; S1 $\{Q\}$ $]|$ means there is a predicate H such that

$$|[\text{ x: int } \{P\}; \text{ S0 } \{H\}]| \quad \text{and} \quad |[\text{ x: int } \{H\}; \text{ S1 } \{Q\}]|$$

– the 'postulate of the concatenation'.

(3) $|[$ x: int
          $\{P\}$
        ; if B0 → S0
             ▯ B1 → S1
          fi
          $\{Q\}$
        $]|$

means

$P \Rightarrow$ B0 ∨ B1   and
$|[$ x: int $\{P \land$ B0$\}$; S0 $\{Q\}$ $]|$ and
$|[$ x: int $\{P \land$ B1$\}$; S1 $\{Q\}$ $]|$

– the 'postulate of the alternative statement'.

(4) $|[$ x: int
          $\{P\}$
        ; do   B0 → S0
             ▯ B1 → S1
          od
          $\{Q\}$
        $]|$

means there is a predicate H and an integer function vf such that

$P \Rightarrow$ H   and
$|[$ x: int $\{H \land$ B0 $\land$ vf = VF$\}$; S0 $\{H \land$ vf < VF$\}$ $]|$ and
$|[$ x: int $\{H \land$ B1 $\land$ vf = VF$\}$; S1 $\{H \land$ vf < VF$\}$ $]|$ and
H ∧ (B0 ∨ B1) $\Rightarrow$ vf ≥ 0   and
H ∧ ¬B0 ∧ ¬B1 $\Rightarrow$ Q

– the 'postulate of the repetitive statement' (also known as 'the invariance theorem for the repetitive statement'). The predicate H is called the 'invariant' of the repetition and the integer function vf the 'variant function'.

*   *   *

Concerning the postulate of the concatenation, the weakest P corresponding to a given Q can be obtained by choosing the weakest H for which |[x: int {H}; S1 {Q}]|, and for this H the weakest P for which |[x: int {P}; S0 {H}]|.

*   *   *

There are two general rules for computing with functional specifications, valid for any S:

(5) From

$$|[\ x: int \ \{P0\}; \ S \ \{Q0\} \ ]|$$

and P1 $\Rightarrow$ P0 and Q0 $\Rightarrow$ Q1

it follows that

$$|[\ x: int \ \{P1\}; \ S \ \{Q1\} \ ]|$$

(6) From

$$|[\ x: int \ \{P0\}; \ S \ \{S0\} \ ]| \ \text{and} \ |[\ x: int \ \{P1\}; \ S \ \{Q1\} \ ]|$$

follow

$$|[\ x: int \ \{P0 \wedge P1\}; \ S \ \{Q0 \wedge Q1\} \ ]| \ \text{and} \ |[\ x: int \ \{P0 \vee P1\}; \ S \ \{Q0 \vee Q1\} \ ]|$$

Referring to (5) we can say that in a functional specification the precondition may be strengthened and the postcondition weakened. In (6) circumstances under which the precondition may be weakened and the postcondition strengthened are indicated.

*   *   *

EXERCISES

E0   In |[x: int {P}; S {Q}]| we may substitute any of the four predicates
x = X, x = abs(X), abs(x) = X and abs(x) = abs(X) for P and Q. In
which of these cases do we get the functional specifications of a
program S which computes the absolute value of a number?

E1   Discuss the functional specification

$$|[\ x, \ y: \text{int } \{x = X\}; \ S \ \{y = Y\} \ ]|$$

E2   Is |[x: int {2 · x ≤ X}; skip {x ≤ X}]| valid?

E3   What does |[x: int {P}; skip {P ∧ Q}]| mean for P and Q?

E4   Show that

$$|[\ x, \ y, \ m: \text{int } \{x \geq 0 \ \wedge \ y \geq 0\}; \ m:= x + y \ \{m \geq x \ \underline{\text{max}} \ y\} \ ]|$$

E5   Determine the weakest P such that

$$|[\ x, \ y, \ m: \text{int } \{P\}; \ m:= x \ \underline{\text{max}} \ y \ \{m > x + y\} \ ]|$$

E6   Determine the weakest P such that

$$|[\ x, \ y, \ z: \text{int}; \ c, \ d: \text{bool } \{P\}; \ S \ \{Q\} \ ]|$$

is satisfied for each of the cases given in the following table:

	S	Q		S	Q
(a)	x:= 3	x = 3	(h)	x:= x − y	x = x − y
(b)	x:= 3	x ≠ y	(i)	x:= 2 ∗ x + 1	x = 2 · x + 1
(c)	x:= 3	true	(j)	c:= c ∧ d	c ≡ c ∧ d
(d)	x:= x + 1	y = 7	(k)	c:= c ∨ d	c ≡ c ∨ d
(e)	x:= y / 2	x = 3	(l)	c:= c ≡ d	c ≡ c ≡ d
(f)	x:= y / 2	true	(m)	x:= y mod z	0 ≤ x < z
(g)	z:= x	z = x min y	(n)	z:= (x + y)/ 2	x < z < y

E7   Give a statement list S such that

$$|[\ x, \ y: \text{int } \{P\}; \ x:= 2 \ast x + y; \ S \ \{P\} \ ]|$$

is satisfied for all P.

E8   Characterize all P for which

$$|[\ x, \ y: \text{int } \{P\}; \ x:= (x − y)/ \ 2; \ x:= 2 \ast x + y \ \{P\} \ ]|$$

E9   Give a few expressions P such that

$$|[\ x,\ y:\ \text{int}\ \{P\};\ y:= x;\ x:= y\ \{P\}\ ]|$$

is satisfied, and also give a few expressions which do not satisfy this.

E10   What does the validity of

$$|[\ x,\ y,\ z:\ \text{int}\ \{P\};\ x:= y;\ x:= z\ \{Q\}\ ]|$$

mean for the pair P, Q? Similarly, what does the validity of

$$|[\ x,\ y,\ z:\ \text{int}\ \{P\};\ x:= z\ \{Q\}\ ]|$$

mean?

E11   Show the equivalence of

$$|[\ x,\ y:\ \text{int}\ \{P\};\ x:= y;\ y:= x\ \{Q\}\ ]|$$
and

$$|[\ x,\ y:\ \text{int}\ \{P\};\ x:= y\ \{Q\}\ ]|$$

E12 Q_E^x is by definition the weakest solution of the equation
P: $|[\ x:\ \text{int}\ \{P\};\ x:= E\ \{Q\}\ ]|$.
$(\underline{E}y: x = E_y^x: P_y^x)$ is a solution of the equation Q: $|[\ x:\ \text{int}\ \{P\}\ ;\ x:= E\ \{Q\}\ ]|$.
Prove this (given that it is the strongest solution).

As far as the assignment statement is concerned, the calculation of preconditions amounts to substitution, and the calculation of postconditions to the more complicated (and less familiar) procedure of parametrizing. This purely technical difference explains why we prefer to deal with programs 'backwards'.

(a)   Determine the strongest Q that satisfies
$|[\ x:\ \text{int}\ \{x \geqq 7\};\ x:= x - 7\ \{Q\}\ ]|$, and for this Q the weakest P
that satisfies $|[\ x:\ \text{int}\ \{P\};\ x:= x - 7\ \{Q\}\ ]|$.

(b)   Determine the strongest Q that satisfies
$|[\ x:\ \text{int}\ \{0 \leqq x < 4\};\ x:= x * x\ \{Q\}\ ]|$, and for this Q the weakest P
that satisfies $|[\ x:\ \text{int}\ \{P\};\ x:= x * x\ \{Q\}\ ]|$.

E13   Prove or refute that for all integer x and y:

(a) $(x + y)\underline{\text{mod}}\ 7\ =\ x\ \underline{\text{mod}}\ 7 + y\ \underline{\text{mod}}\ 7$

(b) $(x + y)\underline{\text{mod}}\ 7\ =\ (x\ \underline{\text{mod}}\ 7 + y\ \underline{\text{mod}}\ 7)\ \underline{\text{mod}}\ 7$

(c) $y = 0\ \underline{\text{cor}}\ (x\ \underline{\text{mod}}\ y)\underline{\text{mod}}\ y\ =\ x\ \underline{\text{mod}}\ y$

(d) $(x + x\ \underline{\text{mod}}\ 2)_{x + x\ \underline{\text{mod}}\ 2}^x\ =\ x + x\ \underline{\text{mod}}\ 2$

(e) $2 *((x - x\ \underline{\text{mod}}\ 2)\underline{\text{div}}\ 2)\ =\ x - x\ \underline{\text{mod}}\ 2$

E14   Show that:

$$|[\ c,\ d:\ \text{bool}\ \{c \equiv C\ \wedge\ (d \equiv D)\}$$
$$;\ c:= (c \equiv d);\ d:= (c \equiv d);\ c:= (c \equiv d)$$
$$\{(c \equiv D)\ \wedge\ (d \equiv C)\}$$
$$]|$$

E15 Show that:

$$|[\ c, d: \text{bool} \ \{c \equiv C\}; \ c:= (c \equiv d); \ c:= (c \equiv d) \ \{c \equiv C\} \ ]|$$

E16 Show that:

$$|[\ x, y, z: \text{int} \ \{x \cdot y = z \ \wedge \ x \ \underline{mod} \ 2 = 0\}; \ x:= x \ / \ 2; \ y:= 2 * y$$
$$\{x \cdot y = z\} \ ]|$$

E17 Determine the weakest Boolean expression B for which

$$|[\ x, y, z: \text{int} \ \{x \cdot y = z \ \wedge \ B\}; \ x:= (x - 1)/ \ 2; \ z:= z - y;$$
$$y:= 2 * y \ \{x \cdot y = z\} \ ]|$$

E18 Determine a Boolean expression B, differing in value from *false*, such that, where P is defined as $n \geq 2 \ \wedge \ (\underline{A} \ d: \ \leq d < N: \ \neg d|x)$, the following is satisfied:

$$|[\ n, x: \text{int} \ \{P \wedge B\}; \ n:= n + 1 \ \{P\} \ ]|$$

Show that $(P \ \wedge \ n^2 > x) \ \Rightarrow \ (\underline{A} \ d: \ 2 \leq d < x: \ \neg \ d|x)$.

E19 Prove that for any P

$$|[\ x: \text{int} \ \{P\}; \ \underline{if} \ \ true \rightarrow x:= 1 \ \underline{0} \ \ true \rightarrow x:= -1 \ \underline{fi} \ \{abs(x) = 1\} \ ]|$$

E20 Solve

$$P: \ |[\ x: \text{int} \ \{P\}; \ \underline{if} \ \ true \rightarrow x:= 1 \ \underline{0} \ \ true \rightarrow x:= -1 \ \underline{fi} \ \{x = 1\} \ ]|$$

E21 Is the statement list $\underline{if} \ x = 1 \rightarrow x:= 1 \ \underline{0} \ \ x = -1 \rightarrow x:= 1 \ \underline{fi}$ a solution of:

$$S: \ |[\ x: \text{int} \ \{x = -X\}; \ S \ \{x = X \ \wedge \ abs(x) = 1\} \ ]|$$

and of

$$S: \ |[\ x: \text{int} \ \{x = -X \ \wedge \ abs(x) = 1\}; \ S \ \{x = X\} \ ]|?$$

E22 Prove that the expressions

```
|[ x: int
  {P}
; if B0 → S0; S2 0 B1 → S1; S2 fi
  {Q}
]|
```

and

```
|[ x: int
  {P}
; if B0 → S0 0 B1 → S1 fi
; S2
  {Q}
]|
```

are equivalent for all predicates P and Q, for all Boolean expressions B0 and B1, and for all statement lists S0, S1 and S2.

E23   Prove that it follows from $|[$ x: int $\{B\}$; S0 $\{B\}$ $]|$ and
$|[$ x: int $\{P\}$; <u>if</u> B $\rightarrow$ S0; S1 <u>fi</u> $\{Q\}$ $]|$ that
$|[$ x: int $\{P\}$; S0; <u>if</u>   B $\rightarrow$ S1 <u>fi</u> $\{Q\}$ $]|$.

E24   Investigate the equivalence of

$$|[\ x,\ y,\ z:\ int\ \{P\};\ \underline{if}\ \ x \geq y \rightarrow S2;\ S0\ \ \square\ \ y \geq x \rightarrow S2;\ S1\ \underline{fi}\ \{Q\}\ ]|$$

and

$$|[\ x,\ y,\ z;\ int\ \{P\};\ S2;\ \underline{if}\ \ x \geq y \rightarrow S0\ \ \square\ \ y \geq x \rightarrow S1\ \underline{fi}\ \{Q\}\ ]|$$

for S2 consecutively skip, x, y:= x + 1, y + 1, and x, y:= y, x.

E25   Prove

```
|[ x, y: int
   {y = 2 · x  ∨  y = − 2 · x + 1}
 ; if  y mod 2 = 0  →  x:= x − y
    ▯  y mod 2 = 1  →  x:= x + y
   fi
 ; y:= y + 1
   {y = 2 · x  ∨  y = − 2 · x + 1}
 ]|
```

E26   P being defined as $x > 0\ \wedge\ y > 0$, find the Boolean expressions B0 and B1 such that

```
|[ x, y: int
   {P}
 ; if B0 → x, y:= y, x  ▯  B1 → x:= x − y fi
   {P}
 ]|
```

Also determine Boolean expressions C0 and C1 such that

```
|[ x, y: int
   {P  ∧  x + 2 · y = D}
 ; if  C0 → x, y:= y, x  ▯  C1 → x:= x − y fi
   {P  ∧  x + 2 · y < D}
 ]|
```

Derive

```
|[ x, y: int
   {P}
 ; do  x < y → x, y:= y, x  ▯  x > y → x − y od
   {P  ∧  x = y}
 ]|
```

E27   Bearing in mind the postulates for the alternative and the repetitive statements, we are frequently challenged to find a not-too-strong Boolean expression B for given predicates P, Q and R, and for a given statement list S, while assuming the validity of $|[$ x: int {Q} S {R} $]|$ such that $|[$ x: int {P ∧ B}; S {R} $]|$ follows. To attain this we must consider solutions of the equation X: P ∧ X ⇒ Q, in particular those solutions whose textual form is a Boolean expression. Check this.

　　　　If a solution cannot be (sufficiently simply) represented as a Boolean expression, we can try to 'simplify' such a solution: if P ∧ Y is a solution, then so is the simpler expression Y; if ¬P ∨ Y is a solution, then again so is the simpler expression Y. Find a Boolean expression B, different from *false*, such that P ∧ B ⇒ Q for

$$P ≡ (\underline{E}\ k: k ≥ 0: 0: x = 2^k) \quad\text{and}\quad Q ≡ (\underline{E}\ k: k ≥ 1: x = 2^k)$$

Also, for

$$P ≡ (r = (\underline{N}\ i: 0 ≤ i < n: X(i) = 0)) \quad\text{and}$$
$$Q ≡ (r = (\underline{N}\ i: 0 ≤ i < n + 1: X(i) = 0)).$$

E28   Calculate Boolean expressions B0, B1 and B2 such that

```
|[ x: int
   {x = X}
 ; if  B0 → x:= − x  ▯  B1 → skip  ▯  B2 → x:= 0 fi
   {x = abs(X)}
 ]|
```

E29   Determine Boolean expressions B0 and B1 such that

```
|[ x, y, z: int
   { x^y · z = C  ∧  x ≥ 1  ∧  y ≥ 1}
 ; if B0  →  x, y:= x * x, y / 2
   ▯ B1  →  x, y, z:= x * x, (y − 1)/ 2, z * x
   fi
   {x^y · z = C  ∧  x ≥ 1  ∧  y ≥ 0}
 ]|
```

E30   Prove that

$$|[\ x, y:\ int\ \{y > 0\};\ \underline{do}\ \ x ≤ 0\ →\ x:= x + y\ \underline{od}\ \{x > 0\}\ ]|$$

E31   Prove that

$$|[\ x, y:\ int\ \{true\};\ \underline{do}\ \ x < y\ →\ x, y:= y, x\ \underline{od}\ \{x ≥ y\}\ ]|$$

and that

```
|[ x, y, z: int
   {true}
 ; do  x < y  →  x, y:= y, x  ▯  y < z  →  y, z:= z, y od
   {x ≥ y  ∧  y ≥ z}
 ]|
```

E32 Does the following hold:

$$|[\ x,\ y:\ int$$
$$\{true\}$$
$$;\ \underline{do}\ \ x < y\ \rightarrow\ x,\ y{:=}\ y,\ x\ \ [\!]\ \ y < x\ \rightarrow\ y,\ x{:=}\ x,\ y,\ \underline{od}$$
$$\{x = y\}$$
$$]|\ ?$$

E33 Are

$$|[\ x:\ int\ \{P\};\ \underline{do}\ \ B0 \rightarrow S\ \ [\!]\ \ B1 \rightarrow S\ \underline{od}\ \{Q\}\ ]|$$

and

$$|[\ x:\ int\ \{P\};\ \underline{do}\ \ B0 \vee B1\ \rightarrow\ S\ \underline{od}\ \{Q\}\ ]|$$

equivalent?

E34 Are

$$|[\ x:\ int\ \{P\};\ \underline{do}\ \ B0 \rightarrow S0\ \ [\!]\ \ B1 \rightarrow S1\ \underline{od}\ \{Q\}\ ]|$$

and

$$|[\ x:\ int\ \{P\};\ \underline{do}\ \ B0 \rightarrow S0\ \ [\!]\ \ B1 \wedge \neg B0\ \rightarrow\ S1\ \underline{od}\ \{Q\}\ ]|$$

equivalent?

E35 From $P \Rightarrow (B0 \vee B1)$ and $|[\ x:\ int\ \{P \wedge B0\};\ S0\ \{P\}\ ]|$ and $|[\ x:\ int\ \{P \wedge B1\};\ S1\ \{P\}\ ]|$, it follows that

$$|[\ x:\ int$$
$$\{P\}$$
$$;\ \underline{do}\ \ B0 \rightarrow S0\ \ [\!]\ \ B1 \rightarrow S1\ \underline{od}$$
$$\{false\}$$
$$]|$$

provided that the repetition terminates.
        Check this. What conclusion may be drawn?

Remark. In quite a different connection we come across this conclusion, amounting to the 'postulate of the excluded termination', as 'the postulate of the excluded deadly embrace'. Deadly embrace (deadlock) concerns the phenomenon in which a number of cooperating (computation) processes have manoeuvred themselves into such a position that for each of the processes any continuation has become impossible.   ∎

E36 Determine the weakest P such that

$$|[\ x:\ int\ \{P\};\ \underline{do}\ \ x \neq 0\ \rightarrow\ x{:=}\ x - 1\ \underline{od}\ \{x = 0\}\ ]|$$

Also determine the weakest P such that

$$|[\ x:\ int\ \{P\};\ \underline{do}\ \ x \neq 0\ \rightarrow\ x{:=}\ x - 2\ \underline{od}\ \{x = 0\}\ ]|$$

Consider

$$|[\text{ x: int } \{P\}; \underline{do} \text{ } x \neq 0 \rightarrow x:= x - 1$$
$$\Box \text{ } x \neq 0 \rightarrow x:= x - 2$$
$$\underline{od}$$
$$\{x = 0\}$$
$$]|$$

E37   Prove that for a Boolean function B(y: y ≥ 0)

$$|[\text{ x: int}$$
$$\{(\underline{E} \text{ y: } y \geq 0: B(y))\}$$
$$; \text{ x:= 0; } \underline{do} \text{ } \neg B(x) \rightarrow x:= x + 1 \text{ } \underline{od}$$
$$\{B(x) \wedge (\underline{A} \text{ z: } 0 \leq z < x: \neg B(z))\}$$
$$]|$$

– the Linear Search Theorem.
Show how with the above program it follows that

$$(\underline{E} \text{ y: } y \geq 0: B(y))$$
$$(\underline{E}y: y \geq 0: B(y) \wedge (\underline{A} \text{ z: } 0 \leq z < y: \neg B(z)))$$

– the postulate of mathematical induction.
The postulates of mathematical induction and of the repetitive statement amount to the same thing for computable Boolean functions. (Note that not all functions are computable: for a sequence of numbers x(i: i ≥ 0) the computation of an n such that n ≥ 0 ∧ (A: n ≤ i: x(i) ≥ 7) causes a lot of worry, even if the existence of such an n is known.)

E38   Let f(x) be a permitted integer expression for any integer x, and let f be increasing. Determine the weakest P such that

$$|[\text{ x: int } \{P\}; \underline{do} \text{ } f(x) > x \rightarrow x:= f(x) \text{ } \underline{od} \text{ } \{f(x) \leq x\}]|$$

E39   Determine the weakest P such that

$$|[\text{ x, y, z: int}$$
$$\{P\}$$
$$; \underline{do} \text{ } x < y \rightarrow x:= x + 1$$
$$\Box \text{ } y < z \rightarrow y:= y + 1$$
$$\Box \text{ } z < x \rightarrow z:= z + 1$$
$$\underline{od}$$
$$\{x = y \wedge y = z \wedge z = x\}$$
$$]|$$

E40   Prove that

$$|[\text{ x, a, b, u, v: int}$$
$$\{a \geq 1 \wedge b \geq 1 \wedge u \geq 0 \wedge v \geq 0 \wedge x = u \cdot a - v \cdot b\}$$
$$; \underline{do} \text{ } x > 0 \rightarrow x, \text{ u:= } x - a, \text{ } u - 1$$
$$\Box \text{ } x < 0 \rightarrow x, \text{ v:= } x + b, \text{ } v - 1$$

$$\underline{\text{od}}$$
$$\{x = 0\}$$
$$]|$$

E41   Prove that

$$|[\ x, y: \text{int}$$
$$\{\text{true}\}$$
$$; \ \underline{\text{do}} \ x > y$$
$$\rightarrow \ \underline{\text{if}} \ \ x \ \underline{\text{mod}} \ \ 2 = 0 \ \lor \ y \ \underline{\text{mod}} \ 2 = 0 \ \rightarrow \ x, \ y:= x - 1, \ y + 1$$
$$\llbracket \ x \ \underline{\text{mod}} \ \ 2 = 1 \ \lor \ y \ \underline{\text{mod}} \ 2 = 1 \ \rightarrow$$
$$x, \ y:= x + x \ \underline{\text{mod}} \ \ 2, \ y + y \ \underline{\text{mod}} \ 2$$
$$\underline{\text{fi}}$$
$$\underline{\text{od}}$$
$$\{x \leq y\}$$
$$]|$$

E42   Show that an inner block with the functional specification

$$|[\ y: \text{int}$$
$$\{x \geq 0\}$$
$$; \ \text{statement list}$$
$$\{y^2 \leq x < (y + 1)^2\}$$
$$; \ b:= (x = y * y)$$
$$]|$$

satisfies

$$S: \ |[\ x: \text{int}; \ b: \text{bool} \ \{x \geq 0\}; \ S \ \{b \ \equiv \ (\underline{E} \ z: z \geq 0: x = z^2)\} \ ]|$$

E43   Which of the texts below are correct functional specifications of a program to compute the smallest N cubes of natural numbers?

(a) $|[\ N: \text{int}; \ f(x: 0 \leq x < N): \underline{\text{array of}} \ \text{int}$
      $\{N \geq 0\}$
      ; cubes
      $\{(\underline{A} \ x: 0 \leq x < N: \ f(x) = x^3)\}$
      $]|$

(b) $|[\ N: \text{int}; \ f(x: 0 \leq x < N): \underline{\text{array of}} \ \text{int}$
      $\{N = N0 \ \land \ N \geq 0\}$
      ; cubes
      $\{N = N0 \ \land \ (\underline{A} \ x: 0 \leq x < N: \ f(x) = x^3)\}$
      $]|$

(c) $|[\ N: \text{int}$
      $\{N \geq 0\}$
      ; $|[\ f(x: 0 \leq x < N): \underline{\text{array of}} \ \text{int}$
         ; cubes
         $\{(\underline{A} \ x: 0 \leq x < N: \ f(x) = x^3)\}$
         $]|$
      $]|$

E44   Give a functional specification of a program to determine the sum of the digits from the decimal representation of a natural number.

2

Programming exercises

This chapter, which forms the heart of Part 1, consists chiefly of a long series of programming exercises. However, the order of the exercises, their presentation, and a possible style of presentation of the solutions will first be discussed.

The exercises are more or less in order of increasing difficulty. This means that the series begins with exercises of which it is fairly firmly established that they belong to the simplest problems, and that the more complicated problems come later. This also means that the level of difficulty, following the series, can fluctuate greatly. The reader should be prepared for this.

Each programming exercise is eventually of the form: Give a statement list for given predicates P and Q, which is a solution of the equation S: |[x: int {P}; S {Q}]|.

In these exercises in which the precondition and postcondition are explicitly given, we only give the equation.

In a great number of exercises we give merely a (verbal) characterization of the desired overall effect of the program to be constructed. In such cases it is also the reader's task to give an explicit formulation of the precondition and postcondition: formulating functional specifications is inextricably linked with programming.

In order to reduce the amount of writing to satisfy proof obligations, and for the sake of compact program presentation, we introduce the abbreviation mechanism known as 'program annotation'. This is best illustrated by an example:

```
|[ N: int
   {N ≥ 0}
 ; |[ a: int
    ; |[ b: int
       ; a, b:= 0, N + 1
         {invariant P:  0 ≤ a < b  ∧  a² ≤ N < b², see Note 0
          variant function: b − a
          }
```

159

```
; do a + 1 ≠ b
  → |[ c: int
     ; c:= (a + b)div 2
       {P ∧ a < c < b, see Note 1}
     ; if c * c ≤ N → a:= c {P, see Note 2}
       ▯ N < c * c → b:= c {P, compare Note 2}
       fi
       {P}
     ]|
  od
  {P ∧ a + 1 = b}
  ]|
  {therefore, a² ≤ N < (a + 1)²}
  ]|
  ]|
```

This program is fully annotated which means that for each of the constituent statements, both the precondition and the postcondition can be deduced from the text. In this way the annotated program shows what must be proved: for each of the statements the given pair of 'boundary conditions' should follow from the postulate going with the statement. Note that each of the proof obligations thus created must be fulfilled.

At the same time we adopt the convention of adding a suggestion in the postcondition for the proof obligations that explicitly require closer attention.

In the example there are five such suggestions, three in the form of a reference to a Note, one (compare Note 2) giving an indication of the form of the proof, and one in the form of a (quite superfluous) therefore.

On the basis of this annotated text, the following must therefore be added:

Note 0   containing the proof of:

$$N ≥ 0 ⇒ P_{0,N+1}^{a,b}$$

Note 1   containing the proof of:

$$P ∧ a + 1 ≠ b ⇒ (P ∧ a < c < b)_{(a+b)div\ 2}^{c}$$

Note 2   containing the proof of:

$$P ∧ a < c < b ∧ c² ≤ N ⇒ P_c^a$$

given which, we consider the example program sufficiently documented.

Termination of repetitive statements will always be dealt with by giving a variant function. In a great many cases the termination proof is trivial (we shall see why later on), and we shall only mention the chosen variant function, as we did in the example. In less trivial cases the termination proof should never be missing.

Remark. Attentive readers will have noticed that this convention for annotated program texts enables us to suppress the mention of any proof by annotating without suggestions – a possibility chosen on purpose for the really trivial programs.

It is one of the characteristics of the best programmers that they are not too quick to consider something as obvious. They know that a lack of awareness of what is and what is not trivial leads immediately to one incorrect program after another.

In this respect the series of exercises below, whether deliberately or not, forms an unusual exercise in mathematical style.   ■

EXERCISES

E0 Write a program that determines whether one of three numbers is the average of the other two.

E1 Write a program that for two numbers p and q, $q \neq 0$, computes a solution of the equation

$$x: \quad x \leq \frac{p}{q} < x + 1$$

E2 Write a program to compute the largest multiple of eight which is, at most, a given number.

E3 Write a program to determine the digits of the representation in base 7 of a natural number smaller than 343.

E4 Given a natural number N, N < 1024, determine the number of zeros with which the decimal representation of N! ends.

E5 S: |[N: int {N ≥ 0}
    ; |[r: int
        ; S
            {r = ($\underline{S}$ i: $0 \leq i < N$: $(-1)^i \cdot i$)}
        ]|
    ]|

E6 S: |[N: int {N ≥ 0}; F(x: $0 \leq x < N$) : <u>array of</u> int
    ; |[r: int
        ; S
            {r = ($\underline{S}$ x: $0 \leq x < N$: $(-1)^x \cdot F(x)$)}
        ]|
    ]|

E7 S: |[N: int {N ≥ 0}; F(x: $0 \leq x < N$): <u>array of</u> int
    ; |[r: int
        ; S

$$\{r = (\underline{S}\ x: 0 \leq x \ \wedge \ x^2 < N: F(x^2))\}$$
$$]|$$
$$]|$$

E8   Write a program that determines whether a given sequence of numbers is monotone.

E9   Prove the correctness of

```
|[ a: int {a ≥ 0}
; |[ q, r: int
   ; q, r:= 0, a + 1
   ; do r ≥ 4
      → |[ x, y: int
         ; x, y:= r div 4, r mod 4
         ; q, r:= q + x, x + y
         ]|
      od
   ; r:= r - 1
     {a = 3 · q + r ∧ 0 ≤ r < 3}
   ]|
  ]|
```

E10   S; |[N, X: int {N ≥ 0}; H(n: 0 ≤ n < N): <u>array of</u> int
       ; |[r: int
         ; S
           $\{r = (\underline{S}\ n: 0 \leq n < N: H(n) \cdot X^n)\}$
         ]|
        ]|

E11   Write a program that determines, for a given number *N*, the smallest solution of the equation

$$k: \quad k \geq 0 \quad \wedge \quad 2^k \geq N$$

E12   The sequence F(x: x ≥ 0) is defined by the recurrence scheme

$$F(0) = 0, \ F(1) = 1$$
$$F(x + 2) = F(x + 1) + F(x) \quad \text{for all x where x ≥ 0.}$$

Write a program that computes F(N) for a given N ≥ 0.

E13   The function C(n: n ≥ 0) is defined by the recurrence scheme

$$C(0) = 0$$
$$C(n) = C(n\ \underline{div}\ 10) + n\ \underline{mod}\ 10 \quad \text{for any n where n ≥ 1}$$

Construct S such that

```
|[ N: int {N ≥ 0}
; |[ c: int
   ; S
```

$$\{c = C(N)\}$$
$$]|$$
$$]|$$

Prove $(\underline{A}\ N: N \geq 0: N \bmod 9 = C(N) \bmod 9)$

E14 Given a sequence $X(i: 0 \leq i < N), N \geq 0$, such that

$$(\underline{A}\ i: 0 \leq i < N: X(i) = 0\ \vee\ X(i) = 1)$$

write a program to compute the value of

$$(\underline{E}\ n: 0 \leq n \leq N: (\underline{A}\ i: 0 \leq i < n: X(i) = 0)\ \wedge$$
$$(\underline{A}\ i: n \leq i < N: X(i) = 1))$$

E15 S: |[N: int $\{N \geq 0\}$
; F(x: $0 \leq x < N$): array of int
$\{(\underline{A}\ x: 0 \leq x < N: F(x) = 0\ \vee\ F(x) = 1)\}$
; |[c: int
; S
$\{c = (\underline{N}\ x, y: 0 \leq x\ 14\ y < N: F(x) < F(y))\}$
]|
]|

E16 S: |[N: int $\{N \geq 0\}$
; F(x: $0 \leq x < N + 1$): array of int
; |[b: bool
; S
$\{b \equiv (\underline{E}\ x: 0 \leq x < N: F(x) = F(N))\}$
]|
]|

E17 Write a program that determines whether the number 7 occurs in a given sequence of numbers.

E18 Write a program that determines the number of different divisors of a positive number.

E19 S: |[r, k: int
$\{r \bmod 2 = 1\ \wedge\ 1 \leq r < 2^k\}$
; |[x: int
; S
$\{x \bmod 2 = 1\ \wedge\ 1 \leq x < 2^k\ \wedge\ (x^3 - r) \bmod 2^k = 0\}$
]|
]|

E20 S: |[N: int $\{N \geq 0\}$; X(i: $0 \leq i < N$): array of int
; |[c: int
; S
$\{c = (\underline{N}\ i, j: 0 \leq i < j < N: X(i) \leq 0\ \wedge\ X(j) \geq 2)\}$
]|
]|

E21   Given that for three ascending sequences F, G, H(i: i $\geq$ 0)

$$(\underline{E}\ i,\ j,\ k:\ i \geq 0\ \wedge\ j \geq 0\ \wedge\ k \geq 0:\ F(i) = G(j) = H(k))$$

write a program to compute the smallest number that occurs in each of the three sequences.

E22   Consider two ascending sequences X(i: 0 $\leq$ i < M + 1) and Y(i: 0 $\leq$ i < N + 1) (M $\geq$ 0 and N $\geq$ 0), with X(M) = Y(N). On a number line M there are red dots, numbered from and including 0 up to and excluding M, and N blue dots, numbered from and including 0 up to and excluding N. The position of a red dot i is given by X(i), and the position of a blue dot j by Y(j). Write a program that determines whether there are a red and a blue dot at a distance of less than 7.

E23   Write a program that determines for an ascending sequence the number of different values occurring in the sequence.

E24   Grigri:

```
|[ N: int {N ≥ 1}
; X(i: 0 ≤ i < N): array of int {X is ascending}
; |[ lp: int
   ; Grigri
      {lp = (MAX i, j: 0 ≤ i ≤ j < N ∧ X(i) = X(j): j − i + 1)}
   ]|
]|
```

E25   Given a sequence X(i): 0 $\leq$ i < N) (N $\geq$ 1), H(i, j) is defined by

$$H(i,\ j)\ =\ (\underline{A}\ k:\ i \leq k < j:\ X(i) = X(k))$$

for 0 $\leq$ i < j $\leq$ N. Write a program to compute

$$(\underline{N}\ i,\ j:\ 0 \leq i < j \leq N:\ H(i,\ j))$$

E26   Write a program that, for a number N $\geq$ 1, determines the period in the decimal representation of 1 / N.

E27   The sequence RF(n: n $\geq$ 0) is defined by means of a natural function f(x: x $\geq$ 0):

$$RF(0) = 0 \qquad RF(n + 1) = f(RF(n)) \qquad \text{for all } n \geq 0.$$

Given that the sequence RF is eventually periodic, that is,

$$(\underline{E}\ i,\ j:\ 0 \leq i < j:\ RF(i) = RF(j))$$

write a program to compute the period of the sequence RF. The restriction is that no local array may be used for this.

E28   Write a program that makes a table of the cubes of the first N natural numbers. The only arithmetic operations permitted in this are addition and subtraction.

E29   The integer function DG(i, j: $0 \leq i < I \land 0 \leq j < J$) is such that for any i: $0 \leq i < I$ the sequence DG(i, j: $0 \leq j < J$) is ascending, and for any j: $0 \leq j < J$ the sequence DG(i, j: $0 \leq i < I$) is descending.

For a given number X it holds that

$$(\underline{E} \ i, j: 0 \leq i < I \land 0 \leq j < J: X = DG(i, j))$$

Write a program that computes a pair (r, s) for which

$$0 \leq r < I \land 0 \leq s < J \land X = DG(r, s)$$

E30   Write a program for a given integer function

$$M(i, j: 0 \leq i < I \land 0 \leq j < J)$$

which computes

$$(\underline{N} \ i, j: 0 \leq i < I \land 0 \leq j < J: M(i, j) \geq 0)$$

in each of the following cases:

(a)   nothing further is known of M,

(b)   M(i, j) is decreasing as a function of i and increasing as a function of j,

(c)   M(i, j) is descending as a function of i and ascending as a function of j.

How do the programs change in order to compute the value of

$$(\underline{N} \ i, j: 0 \leq i < I \land 0 \leq j < J: M(i, j) = 0)$$

E31   S: |[M, N: int {M $\geq$ 0 $\land$ N $\geq$ 0}
        ; F(i: $0 \leq i < M$), G(j: $0 \leq j < N$): <u>array of</u> int
          {(F is ascending) $\land$ (G is ascending)}
        ; |[c: int
            ; S
              {c = (<u>N</u> i, j: $0 \leq i < M \land 0 \leq j < N$:
                      F(i) + G(j) > 0)}
          ]|
        ]|

E32   S: |[N: int {N $\geq$ 0}
        ; U(i: $0 \leq i < N$): <u>array of</u> int
          {(<u>A</u> i: $0 \leq i < N$: U(i) > 0)}
        ; |[r: int
            ; S
              {r = (<u>N</u> j, k: $0 \leq j \leq N \land 0 \leq k \leq N$:
                      (<u>S</u> i: $0 \leq i < j$: U(i)) =
                      (<u>S</u> i: $k \leq i < N$: U(i)))}
          ]|
        ]|

E33   By means of two integer numbers X and Y, the sequence F(i: $i \geq 0$) is defined by

$$F(0) = 1, F(1) = 1$$
$$F(i + 2) = X \cdot F(i) + Y \cdot F(i + 1) \qquad \text{for all } i \geq 0$$

Give a solution for

```
Fibolucci:
      |[ N: int {N ≥ 1}
    ; |[ r: int
        ; Fibolucci
          {r = (S i: 0 ≤ i ≤ N: F(i) · F(N − i))}
        ]|
      ]|
```

E34 Write a program that determines whether there is a number which occurs in each of two given ascending number sequences (the coincidence test).

E35 A segment $X(i: p \leq i < q)$ of $X(i: 0 \leq i < N)$ is 'left minimal' means

$$0 \leq p < q \leq N \land (\underline{A} \, i: p \leq i < q: X(p) \leq X(i))$$

Write a program to compute the maximal length of any left minimal segment of a given sequence $X(i: 0 \leq i < N), N \geq 1$.

E36 A segment $X(i: p \leq i < q)$ of $X(i: 0 \leq i < N)$ is 'almost ascending' means

$$0 \leq p < q \leq N \land (\underline{N} \, i: p < i < q: X(i - 1) > X(i)) \leq 1$$

Write a program to compute the maximal length of any almost ascending segment of a given sequence $X(i: 0 \leq i < N), N \geq 1$.

E37 A segment $X(i: p \leq i < q)$ of $X(i: 0 \leq i < N)$ is a 'K segment' means

$$0 \leq p < q \leq N \land (\underline{A} \, i, j: p \leq i < q \land p \leq j < q: X(i) \cdot X(j) \geq 0)$$

Write a program to compute the maximal length of any K segment of a given sequence $X(i: 0 \leq i < N), N \geq 1$.

E38 A segment $X(i: p \leq i < q)$ of $X(i: 0 \leq i < N)$ is a 'smooth segment' means

$$0 \leq p < q \leq N \land (\underline{A} \, i, j: p \leq i < q \land p \leq j < q: X(i) - X(j) \leq 1)$$

Write a program to compute the maximal length of any smooth segment of a given sequence $X(i: 0 \leq i < N), N \geq 1$.

E39 A segment $X(i: p \leq i < q)$ of $X(i: 0 \leq i < N)$ is an 'M segment' means

$$0 \leq p < q \leq N \land (\underline{N} \, z: z \text{ integer}: (\underline{E} \, i: p \leq i < q: z = X(i))) \leq 47$$

Write a program to compute the maximal length of any M segment of a given sequence $X(i: 0 \leq i < N), N \geq 1$.

E40   A segment $X(i: p \le i < q)$ of $X(i: 0 \le i < N)$ is a 'dip segment' means

$$0 \le p < q \le N \wedge (\underline{A}\ i, j: p \le i \le j < q: X(i) \le X(j) + 1)$$

Write a program to compute the maximal length of any dip segment of a given sequence $X(i: 0 \le i < N), N \ge 1$.

E41   Write a program that, for given $N \ge 0$, computes the value of

$$(\underline{N}\ x, y: 0 \le x \le y: x^2 + y^2 = N)$$

E42   S: $|[$ N, U: int $\{N \ge 0 \wedge U \ge 0\}$
       ; X(i: $0 \le i < N$): <u>array of</u> int
         { X is ascending }
       ; $|[$ r: int
          ; S
            $\{r = (\underline{N}\ i, j: 0 \le i \le j < N: X(j) - X(i) \le U)\}$
          $]|$
       $]|$

E43   The Boolean function $B(x)$ is defined for all integer x and has in at least one point the value *true*. Write a program that determines such a point. (The expression $B(x)$ may be regarded as a Boolean expression.)

E44   Write a program such that

    $|[$ N: int $\{N \ge 0 \wedge N = NO\}$
    ;X(i: $0 \le i < N$): <u>array of</u> int
      $\{(\underline{A}\ i: 0 \le i < N: X(i) = 0 \vee X(i) = 1)\}$
    ; S
      $\{(X \text{ is ascending}) \wedge N = NO\}$
    $]|$

is satisfied. The restriction here is that the only operations permitted on the array X are X: swap(i, j), where $0 \le i < N$ and $0 \le j < N$.

E45   Consider a function $f(x: 0 \le x < N)$ for which

$$(\underline{A}\ x: 0 \le x < N: 0 \le f(x) < N)$$

In a country there are N places, numbered from 0 up to and including $N - 1$. When a gong is sounded, a person who is in place x instantaneously goes to place $f(x)$. There are two persons, C and D. C, who carries a flaming torch, is originally in place c, and D, with gunpowder, in place d. The gong is sounded an unlimited number of times.

Write a program that assigns the correct value to the Boolean variable bang.

Also write a program for the case in which C moves according to a function f and D according to a function g with

$$(\underline{A}\ x: 0 \le x < N: 0 \le g(x) < N)$$

E46 An integer function $K(i, j: i \geq 0 \wedge j \geq 0)$ is increasing in both arguments. Write a program to compute

$$(\underline{N} \; i, j: i \geq 0 \; \wedge \; j \geq 0: 0 \leq K(i, j) < 47)$$

E47 The syntactic category h is defined by

$$\langle h \rangle ::= 0 \mid 1 \langle h \rangle \langle h \rangle$$

Construct a program S such that

```
|[ N: int {N ≥ 0}
; X(i: 0 ≤ i < 2 · N + 1): array of int
   {(A i: 0 ≤ i < 2 · N + 1: X(i) = 0  ∨  X(i) = 1)}
; |[ b: bool
   ; S
      { b ≡ (X belongs to the category h)}
   ]|
]|
```

Also give an S for the case that h is given by

$$\langle h \rangle ::= 0 \mid \langle h \rangle \, 1 \, \langle h \rangle$$

E48 The sequence $fusc(n: \geq 0)$ is defined by $fusc(0) = 0$, $fusc(1) = 1$, and for all $n \geq 0$ $fusc(2 \cdot n) = fusc(n)$ and $fusc(2 \cdot n + 1) = fusc(n) + fusc(n + 1)$. Determine an S such that

```
|[ N: int {N ≥ 0}
; |[ x: int; S {x = fusc(N)} ]|
]|
```

E49 The set W is defined by

(a) 0 belongs to W,
(b) if x belongs to W, then so do $2 \cdot x + 1$ and $3 \cdot x + 1$,
(c) all elements of W belong to W on the basis of (a) or (b).

Write a program to compute the smallest N elements of W, for given $N \geq 1$.

E50 The superposition of a collection of intervals on a number line is that part of the line covered by these intervals. The length of such a superposition is the length of all that is black after the superposition on an originally white number line is painted black.
   Write a program segment S such that

```
|[ N: int {N ≥ 0}
; X, Y(i: 0 ≤ i < N): array of int
   {(X is ascending)  ∧  (A i: 0 ≤ i < N: X(i) ≤ Y(i))}
; |[ l: int
   ; S
      {l = the length of the superposition of the intervals
           (X(i), Y(i)), 0 ≤ i < N}
   ]|
]|
```

E51   Given the positive integer A and a sequence f(i: i ≥ 0) of natural numbers, such that

$$(\underline{E}\,n: n \geq 0: (\underline{A}\,i: 0 \leq i < n: f(i) \leq A)\ \wedge\ (\underline{A}\,i: n \leq i: f(i) > A))$$

Write a program to compute

$$(\underline{N}\ i, j: 0 \leq i < j: A = (\underline{S}\,k: i \leq k < j: f(k)))$$

Further, write a program for the special case in which f(i) = i for all i ≥ 0.

E52   The N vertices of a polygon are numbered clockwise from and including 0 to N. The distance from vertex i to its clockwise neighbour is d(i), d(i) > 0. Write a program to determine a pair of vertices that halves the perimeter as close as possible.

E53   S: |[M, N: int {M ≥ 0 ∧ N ≥ 0}
         ; K(i: 0 ≤ i < M): <u>array of</u> int
         ; |[b: bool
           ; S
             {b ≡ (<u>A</u> n: 0 ≤ n < N:
                 (<u>E</u> m: 0 ≤ m < M: K(m) = n))}
              ]|
           ]|

E54   The N nodes of a directed graph are numbered from and including 0 to N, N ≥ 1. The branches are given by two arrays p, q(i: 0 ≤ i < N): for all (i, j), 0 ≤ i < N ∧ 0 ≤ j < N, there is a branch from i to j

$$\equiv (i < j\ \wedge\ (p(i) = j\ \vee\ q(i) = j))$$

Write a program to compute the number of paths (in the graph) from node 0 to node N − 1.

E55   For the sequence X(i: 0 ≤ i < N), N ≥ 0, it is given that

$$(\underline{A}\,i: 0 \leq i < N: X(i) = 0\ \vee\ X(i) = 1)$$

A segment X(i: p ≤ i < q) of X(i: 0 ≤ i < N) is 'balanced' means

$$0 \leq p \leq q \leq N \wedge (\underline{N}\,i: p \leq i < q: X(i) = 0)\ =$$
$$(\underline{N}\,i: p \leq i < q: X(i) = 1)$$

Write a program to compute the maximum length of any balanced segment of X(i: 0 ≤ i < N).

E56   Along a circular racetrack there are N pits, numbered clockwise from and including 0 to N. In pit i there is a quantity of petrol, p(i). The amount of petrol necessary to have a racing car span the distance from pit i to the clockwise neighbouring pit equals q(i). Given two sequences of positive numbers p, q(i: 0 ≤ i < N), for which

$$(\underline{S}\ i: 0 \leq i < N: p(i)) = (\underline{S}\ i: 0 \leq i < N: q(i))$$

write a program that computes how many pits a racing car with an originally empty, but sufficiently large, tank must visit to go round the track.

E57   Given two sequences X, Y(i: $0 \leq i < N$), write a program that determines the lexicographic order of X and Y, i.e. whether $X < Y$, $X = Y$ or $X > Y$.

E58   The ascending sequences of positive numbers with sum N can be ordered lexicographically. Write a program that transforms such a sequence, which is not the last one lexicographically, into its successor.

E59   Given a natural function f(x, y: $x \geq 0 \ \wedge \ y \geq 0$) which satisfies

(i) $f(x, y) > x$ for all x and y
(ii) $y1 > y0 \implies f(x, y1) > f(x, y0)$ for all x, y0 and y1,

write a program that computes for a given $N \geq 1$ the smallest N elements of the set V defined by:

(a)   0 belongs to V,
(b)   if x and y belong to V, then f(x, y) also belongs to V,
(c)   all elements which belong to V belong to V on the basis of (a) or (b).

E60   The positive function C(x, y: $x \geq 1 \ \wedge \ y \geq 0$) is defined by the recurrence scheme

$$C(1, y) = 1 \quad \text{for all } y \geq 0$$
$$C(x + 1, y) = C(x, y) \quad \text{for all } x, y \text{ with } x \geq 1 \text{ and } 0 \leq y \leq x$$
$$C(x + 1, y) = C(x, y) + C(x + 1, y - (x + 1)) \quad \text{for all } x, y \text{ with } x < y \text{ and } x \geq 1$$

Write a program that computes the value of C(N, N) for a given $N \geq 1$.

E61   A (non-empty, finite) tree is given by:

(a)   vertex r is the root of the tree,
(b)   a vertex x of the tree has n(x) sons, namely the vertices s(x, i) with $0 \leq i < n(x)$.

A leaf is a vertex of the tree with no sons.
     Write a program that determines the number of leaves of the tree (tip count).

E62   Given an integer K, $K \geq 0$, and an integer array x(i: $0 \leq i < N$), write a program to compute the maximum length of any continuous subsequence of X that contains at most K zeros. The restriction here is that the elements of X may be investigated only once.

E63   Given a matrix of which all elements are 0 or 1, write a program to compute the maximum size of any square submatrix of which all elements are equal to 0.

E64   Consider two integer arrays X, Y(i: $0 \leq i < 47$). In the plane there are 47 points, numbered from and including 0 to 46. Point i has (X(i), Y(i)) as Cartesian coordinates.

A robot makes a tour of the points in order of increasing number, and from point 46 it returns to point 0 again. In so doing it observes the following rules:

(a)   it starts from point 0 looking in the direction of point 1,
(b)   it always goes in the direction in which it is looking,
(c)   it changes its direction only in the points i, by a rotation to the right over an angle smaller than 360°,
(d)   it ends in point 0 looking in the direction of point 1.

As a consequence of this tour the robot makes an integer number of complete (clockwise) rotations.

Write a program to calculate this number, with the restriction that any expression in the program must be of the type *integer* or *Boolean*.

3
Solutions to selected exercises

The following solutions are included to illustrate the possible style of presentation.

Section 0.0

E3 $(\neg P \lor Q) \;\land\; (P \lor R)$

=   {distribution of conjunction over disjunction}

$((\neg P \lor Q) \land P) \;\lor\; ((\neg P \lor Q) \land R)$

=   {complement rules}

$(Q \land P) \;\lor\; ((\neg P \lor (P \land Q)) \land R)$

=   {distribution of conjunction over disjunction}

$(Q \land P) \;\lor\; (\neg P \land R) \;\lor\; (P \land Q \land R)$

=   {absorption rule}

$(Q \land P) \;\lor\; (\neg P \land R)$

E16 The domains for the dummies i and j are constant as long as the argument lasts. We shall leave them anonymous.

$(\underline{A} \; i:: (\underline{A} \; j:: X(i) \cdot X(j) \geq 0))$

=   {arithmetic}

$(\underline{A} \; i:: (\underline{A} \; j:: (X(i) \geq 0 \;\lor\; X(j) \leq 0) \;\land\; (X(i) \leq 0 \;\lor\; X(j) \geq 0)))$

= $\{(\underline{A} \; j:: P \land Q) \;\equiv\; (\underline{A} \; j:: P) \;\land\; (\underline{A} \; j:: Q)\}$

$(\underline{A} \; i:: (\underline{A} \; j:: X(i) \geq 0 \;\lor\; X(j) \leq 0)$

$\land \;\; (\underline{A} \; j:: X(i) \leq 0 \;\lor\; X(j) \geq 0)$

$)$

= $\{(\underline{A} \; i:: P \land Q) \;\equiv\; (\underline{A} \; i:: P) \;\land\; (\underline{A} \; i:: Q)\}$

$(\underline{A} \; i:: (\underline{A} \; j:: X(i) \geq 0 \;\lor\; X(j) \leq 0))$

$\land \;\; (\underline{A} \; i:: (\underline{A} \; j:: X(i) \leq 0 \;\lor\; X(j) \geq 0))$

=   {symmetry}

$$(\underline{A}\ i::\ (\underline{A}\ j::\ X(i) \geq 0 \quad \vee \quad X(j) \leq 0))$$
$$= \quad \{j \text{ does not occur in } X(i) \geq 0\}$$
$$(\underline{A}\ i::\ X(i) \geq 0 \quad \vee \quad (\underline{A}\ j::\ X(j) \leq 0))$$
$$= \quad \{i \text{ does not occur in } (\underline{A}\ j::\ X(j) \leq 0)\}$$
$$(\underline{A}\ i::\ X(i) \geq 0) \quad \vee \quad (\underline{A}\ j::\ X(j) \leq 0)$$

Section 0.3

E1   (c)   On the basis of

$$X \vee (P \wedge Q) \quad \Rightarrow \quad Q$$
$$= \quad \{\text{definition} \Rightarrow\}$$
$$\neg(X \vee (P \wedge Q)) \quad \vee \quad Q$$
$$= \quad \{\text{de Morgan}\}$$
$$(\neg X \wedge (\neg P \vee \neg Q)) \quad \vee \quad Q$$
$$= \quad \{\text{distribution of disjunction over conjunction}\}$$
$$(\neg X \vee Q) \quad \wedge \quad (\neg P \vee \neg Q \vee Q)$$
$$= \quad \{\text{elementary}\}$$
$$\neg X \vee Q$$
$$= \quad \{\text{definition} \Rightarrow\}$$
$$X \quad \Rightarrow \quad Q$$

the given equation can be rewritten as

$$X:\ X \Rightarrow Q$$

with Q as its weakest solution.

E6   For each pair of sequences $f, g(i: 0 \leq i < N)$ it holds that

$$\neg(f < g) \quad \wedge \quad \neg(g < f)$$
$$= \quad \{\text{ definition lexicographic ordering; de Morgan}\}$$
$$(\underline{A} \quad x: 0 \leq x < N: f(x) \geq g(x) \quad \vee \quad (\underline{E}\ y: 0 \leq y < x: f(y) \neq g(y)))$$

$$\wedge$$

$$(\underline{A} \quad x: 0 \leq x < N: g(x) \geq f(x) \quad \vee \quad (\underline{E}\ y: 0 \leq y < x: g(y) \neq f(y)))$$
$$= \quad \{(\underline{A}\ x: P: Q) \wedge (\underline{A}\ x: P: R) \quad \equiv \quad (\underline{A}\ x: P: Q \wedge R)\}$$
$$(\underline{A} \quad x: 0 \leq x < N:(f(x) \geq g(x) \quad \vee \quad (\underline{E}\ y: 0 \leq y < x: f(y) \neq g(y)))$$
$$\wedge (g(x) \geq f(x) \quad \vee \quad (\underline{E}\ y: 0 \leq y < x: g(y) \neq f(y)))$$
$$)$$
$$= \quad \{ \text{ distribution disjunction over conjunction; arithmetic}\}$$

$$(\underline{A} \quad x: 0 \leq x < N: f(x) = g(x) \quad \vee \quad (\underline{E} \ y: 0 \leq y < x:$$
$$f(y) \neq g(y)))$$
$$= \quad \{\text{complete induction}\}$$
$$(\underline{A} \quad x: 0 \leq x < N: f(x) = g(x))$$
$$= \quad \{\text{definition equality of sequences}\}$$
$$(f = g)$$

Section 1

E4   Since

$$|[\ x, y, m: int\ \{x \geq 0\ \wedge\ y \geq 0\};\ m:= x + y\ \{m \geq x\ \underline{max}\ y\}\ ]|$$

holds,

$$x \geq 0 \wedge y \geq 0\ \Rightarrow\ (m \geq x\ \underline{max}\ y)^m_{x+y}$$

must be satisfied, and this is so because

$$(m \geq x\ \textbf{max}\ y)^m_{x+y}$$
$$= \quad \{\text{definition} \quad R^x_E\}$$
$$x + y \geq x\ \textbf{max}\ y$$
$$\{\text{definition}\ x\ \textbf{max}\ y\}$$
$$x + y \geq x\ \wedge\ x + y \geq y$$
$$= \quad \{\text{arithmetic}\}$$
$$x \geq 0\ \wedge\ y \geq 0$$

E8   On the basis of the rules of concatenation and assignment, the validity of

$$|[\ x, y: int\ \{P\};\ x:= (x - y)/\ 2;\ x:= 2 * x + y\ \{P\}\ ]|$$

means that P satisfies

$$P\ \Rightarrow\ (x - y\ even)\ \wedge\ (P^x_{2 \cdot x + y})^x_{(x - y)/2}$$

or, because $(P^x_{2 \cdot x + y})^x_{(x-y)/2} \equiv P$, that it satisfies

$$P\ \Rightarrow\ (x - y\ even)\ \wedge\ P$$

or

$$P\ \Rightarrow\ (x - y\ even)$$

E26   On the basis of the rules of alternative statement and assignment, the validity of

$$|[\ x, y: int$$
$$\{P\};\ \underline{if}\ B0 \to x, y:= y, x\ [\!]\ B1 \to x:= x - y\ \underline{fi}\ \{P\}$$
$$]|$$

means that each of the following conditions is satisfied:

$$P \Rightarrow B0 \vee B1$$
$$\text{(i)} \quad P \wedge B0 \Rightarrow P^{x,y}_{y,x}$$
$$\text{(ii)} \quad P \wedge B1 \Rightarrow P^{x}_{x-y}$$

Where P is defined by $P \equiv x > 0 \wedge y > 0$, this means for the Boolean expressions B0 and B1 that they must satisfy each of the following conditions:

$$x > 0 \wedge y > 0 \Rightarrow B0 \vee B1$$
$$x > 0 \wedge y > 0 \wedge B0 \Rightarrow y > 0 \wedge x > 0$$
$$x > 0 \wedge y > 0 \wedge B1 \Rightarrow x - y > 0 \wedge y > 0$$

This is satisfied, for example, by choosing *true* for B0 and $x > y$ for B1.

$$* \quad * \quad *$$

The validity of

```
|[ x, y: int
   {P  ∧  x + 2 · y = D}
 ; if  C0 → x, y:= y, x  ▯  C1 → x:= x − y  fi
   {x + 2 · y < D}
]|
```

means that each of the following conditions is satisfied:

$$P \wedge x + 2 \cdot y = D \Rightarrow C0 \vee C1$$
$$\text{(iii)} \quad P \wedge x + 2 \cdot y = D \wedge C0 \Rightarrow (x + 2 \cdot y < D)^{x,y}_{y,x}$$
$$\text{(iv)} \quad P \wedge x + 2 \cdot y = D \wedge C1 \Rightarrow (x + 2 \cdot y < D)^{x}_{x-y}$$

With P again defined by $P \equiv x > 0 \wedge y > 0$, this is satisfied by taking $x < y$ for C0 and *true* for C1.

$$* \quad * \quad *$$

Taking the conjunction of (i) with (iii) and of (ii) with (iv) yields

$$P \wedge x + 2 \cdot y = D \wedge B0 \wedge C0 \Rightarrow (P \wedge x + 2 \cdot y < D)^{x,y}_{y,x}$$
$$P \wedge x + 2 \cdot y = D \wedge B1 \wedge C1 \Rightarrow (P \wedge x + 2 \cdot y < D)^{x}_{x-y}$$

or, with the choices made for B0, B1, C0 and C1,

$$P \wedge x + 2 \cdot y = D \wedge x < y \Rightarrow (P \wedge x + 2 \cdot y < D)^{x,y}_{y,x}$$

and

$$P \wedge x + 2 \cdot y = D \wedge x > y \Rightarrow (P \wedge x + 2 \cdot y < D)^{x}_{x-y}$$

from which, together with the validity of

$$P \wedge (x < y \vee x > y) \Rightarrow x + 2 \cdot y \geq 0$$

it follows from the postulate of the repetitive statement (invariant P, variant function $x + 2 \cdot y$) that:

```
|[ x, y: int
   {P}
 ; do  x < y → x, y:= y, x  ▯  x > y → x:= x - y od
   {P  ∧  x = y}
]|
```

Section 2

E13   The given functional specification is satisfied with the following inner block for **S**

```
|[ n: int {N ≥ 0}
 ; c:= 0; n:= N
   {invariant P: 0 ≤ n ≤ N  ∧  c + C(n) = C(N), see Note 0.
   variant function: n
   }
 ; do n ≠ 0
      → c:= c + n mod  10; n:= n div 10 {P, see Note 2}
   od
   { c = C(N), see Note 1}
]|
```

Note 0. The validity of $N \geq 0 \implies (P_N^n)_0^c$ follows from

$$(P_N^n)_0^c$$
$$= \quad \{\text{definition } P\}$$
$$0 \leq N \leq N \quad \wedge \quad 0 + C(N) = C(N)$$
$$= \quad \{\text{calculus}\}$$
$$0 \leq N$$

Note 1. The validity of $P \quad \wedge \quad n = 0 \implies c = C(N)$ follows from

$$P \quad \wedge \quad n = 0$$
$$\implies \quad \{\text{definition } P\}$$
$$c + C(0) = C(N)$$
$$= \quad \{\text{definition } C\}$$
$$c = C(N)$$

Note 2. The validity of $P \quad \wedge \quad n \neq 0 \implies (P_{n \text{ div } 10}^n)_{c + n \text{ mod } 10}^c$ follows from

$$(P^n_{n \text{ div } 10})^c_c + n \text{ mod } 10$$
$=$ {definition P}
$0 \leq n \text{ div } 10 \leq N \quad \wedge \quad c + n \text{ mod } 10 + C(n \text{ div } 10) = C(N)$
$\Leftarrow$ {arithmetic and definition C}
$c + C(n) = C(N) \quad \wedge \quad 1 \leq n \leq N$
$\Leftarrow$ {definition P}
$P \quad \wedge \quad n \neq 0$

That the repetition terminates follows from the validity of

$$P \implies n \geq 0$$

(which expresses that the variant function has a lower bound), and from the validity of

$$P \quad \wedge \quad n \neq 0 \quad \wedge \quad n = VF \implies ((n < VF)^n_{n \text{ div } 10})^c_c + n \text{ mod } 10$$

(which expresses that the variant function drops effectively), following from

$$((n < VF)^n_{n \text{ div } 10})^c_c + n \text{ mod } 10$$
$=$ {substitution}
$n \text{ div } 10 < VF$
$\Leftarrow$ {definition div}
$n > 0 \quad \wedge \quad n = VF$
$\Leftarrow$ {definition P}
$P \quad \wedge \quad n \neq 0 \quad \wedge \quad n = VF$

Two objections

- The assertion that a given program text satisfies a given functional specification should be understood as a mathematical theorem, and therefore requires a proof.

    In this sense the above presentation has an extremely familiar and traditional form: first the program is given, and then there follows the correctness proof. All kinds of circumstances are conceivable (but which will not be discussed here), under which such a style of program documentation is quite practical. If, however, the aim is to design programs, i.e. to design mathematical theorems, then this form of transfer is perhaps too thorough, since the *quo modo* is hardly mentioned. We shall gradually pay more attention to this in the elaboration of the following exercises.

- The above correctness proof is given in about the greatest detail that the system of reasoning described here allows.

This makes the discussion of such a simple little program unduly long. We have, indeed, only given the proof thus extensively by way of illustration. As the reader becomes more experienced, the detailed steps of our proofs will be gradually and homogeneously diminished, never losing sight of the fact that, if challenged, we must always be able to give a proof in all its relevant detail.   ∎

The reader should verify that the relation

$(c + n) \underline{\mod} \ 9 = N \underline{\mod} \ 9$

is an invariant for the repetition of the given program. From this it follows, together with P and $n = 0$ that $C(N) \underline{\mod} \ 9 = N \underline{\mod} \ 9$.

E25 A functional specification of the program to be constructed is

```
S:  |[ N: int {N ≥ 1}; X(i: 0 ≤ i < N): array of int
    ; |[ c: int
       ; S
         {R:  c = (N i, j: 0 ≤ i < j ≤ N: H(i, j))}
       ]|
    ]|
```

In this R is the name for the desired postcondition, and $H(i, j)$ is a predicate which is defined for all i, j with $0 \le i < j \le N$ by $H(i, j) \equiv (\underline{A} \ k: i \le k < j: X(i) = X(k))$.

For S, choose an inner block with repetition. As invariant of the repetition choose P, defined by

$P \equiv 1 \le n \le N \ \land \ c = (\underline{N} \ i, j: 0 \le i < j \le n: H(i, j))$

and obtained from R by replacing the constant N in R by the variable n.

Projected on n, S looks like

$|[\ n: \text{int}; \ n := 1; \ \underline{do} \ n \ne N \ \to \ n := n + 1 \ \underline{od} \ ]|$

so that termination is guaranteed (variant function $N - n$).

Since, using $P \land n \ne N$

$(\underline{N} \ i, j: 0 \le i < j \le n + 1: H(i, j))$
= {splitting off the term with $j = n + 1$, which is permitted because of $1 \le n + 1 \le N$, following from $P \land n \ne N$}
$(\underline{N} \ i, j: 0 \le i < j \le n: H(i, j))$
$+ (\underline{N} \ i: 0 \le i < n + 1: H(i, n + 1))$
= {with P}
$c + (\underline{N} \ i: 0 \le i < n + 1: H(i, n + 1))$

projected on n and c, S looks like:

```
|[ n: int
; n:= 1; c:= 1 {P}
; do n ≠ N → c:= c + d; n:= n + 1 od
]|
```

provided that the precondition of c:= c + d can be strengthened with

$$d = (\underline{N}\ i: 0 \le i < n + 1: H(i, n + 1))$$

This strengthening can be achieved by strengthening the invariant to $P \wedge Q$, where W is defined by

$$Q \equiv d = (\underline{N}\ i: 0 \le i < n: H(i, n))$$

Since, using $P \wedge Q \wedge n \ne N$:

$(\underline{N}\ i: 0 \le i < n + 1: H(i, n + 1))$

= {splitting off the term with $i = n$, which is permitted because of $1 \le n + 1 \le N$, following from $P \wedge n \ne N$}

$(\underline{N}\ i: 0 \le i < n: H(i, n + 1)) + (\underline{N}\ i: 0 \le i = n: H(n, n + 1))$

= {with the definition of H}

$(\underline{N}\ i: 0 \le i < n: H(i, n) \quad \wedge \quad X(i) = X(n)) +$
$\qquad\qquad\qquad\qquad\qquad (\underline{N}\ i: 0 \le i = n:$
$\qquad\qquad\qquad\qquad\qquad\quad true)$

= {Remark below + calculus}

$(\underline{N}\ i: 0 \le i < n: H(i, n) \quad \wedge \quad X(n - 1) = X(n)) + 1$

= {calculus}

if $X(n - 1) = X(n) \quad \rightarrow \quad (\underline{N}\ i: 0 \le i < n: H(i, n)) + 1$
▌ $X(n - 1) \ne X(n \quad \rightarrow \quad (\underline{N}\ i: 0 \le i < n: false) + 1$
fi

= {with Q}

if $X(n - 1) = X(n) \rightarrow d + 1 \quad ▌ \quad X(n - 1) \ne X(n) \rightarrow$
1 **fi**

projected on n, c and d, S looks like:

```
|[ n, d: int
;    n:= 1, c:= 1 {P}; d:= 1 {P ∧ Q}
; do n ≠ N
      → {P ∧ Q ∧ n ≠ N}
        if X(n - 1) = X(n) → d:= d + 1
        ▌ X(n - 1) ≠ X(n) → d:= 1
        fi
        {P ∧ Qⁿₙ₊₁}
   ; c:= c + d
```

$$\{P^n_{n+1} \ \wedge \ Q^n_{n+1}\}$$
$$; \ n := n + 1$$
$$\{P \wedge Q\}$$
od
$$\{P \ \wedge \ n = N, \text{ therefore } R\}$$
]|

Note. Since it holds for $0 \le i < n$ that

$$H(i, n) \ \equiv \ H(i, n) \ \wedge \ X(i) = X(n - 1) \tag{1}$$

we conclude

$$H(i, n) \ \wedge \ X(i) = X(n)$$
$$= \ \{(1)\}$$
$$H(i, n) \ \wedge \ X(i) = X(n - 1) \ \wedge \ X(i) = X(n)$$
$$= \ \{\text{arithmetic}\}$$
$$H(i, n) \ \wedge \ X(i) = X(n - 1) \ \wedge \ X(n - 1) = X(n)$$
$$= \ \{(1)\}$$
$$H(i, n) \ \wedge \ X(n - 1) = X(n) \qquad \blacksquare$$

Remarks.

(a)   The way in which P is obtained from R is quite often applicable (and by now standard).

(b)   The way in which Q is obtained from P is also quite often applicable (and by now standard): Q registers the change in c necessary to retain P when n increments by 1. (Informally, Q is sometimes called the first derivative of P.)

(c)   We could have substituted the calculation executed in the above Note into the relevant computation. This, however, would have given rise to quite a lot of copying, since the formula which is manipulated in the above Note is only a small part of the formula in which it is embedded.

(d)   The little theorem proved in this Note is so very trivial that it must be questioned whether it should be proved in such detail.   ■

E30   (c)   With C defined by

$$C = (\underline{N} \ i, j: 0 \le i < I \ \wedge \ 0 \le j < J: M(i, j) \ge 0)$$

we construct a program S such that the following is satisfied:

```
|[ I, J: int {I ≥ 0  ∧  J ≥ 0}
; M(i, j: 0 ≤ i < I  ∧  0 ≤ j < J): array of int
  {(A i: 0 ≤ i < I: M(i, j: 0 ≤ j < J) is ascending)
   ∧ (A j: 0 ≤ j < J: M(i, j: 0 ≤ i < I) is descending)}
; |[ c: int
```

```
    ; S
      {R: c = C}
    ]|
  ]|
```

For **S** we choose an inner block with repetition, and for the invariant the relation **P** is defined by

$$P \equiv (0 \leq m \leq I \;\wedge\; 0 \leq n \leq J$$
$$\wedge\; C = c + (\underline{\text{N}}\; i,\, j:\, m \leq i < I \,\wedge\, n \leq j < J:\, M(i,\, j) \geq 0)$$
$$)$$

Since the initialization of **P** is easy for m and n both zero, and since

$$P \;\wedge\; (m = I \;\vee\; n = J) \;\Rightarrow\; R$$

we investigate ways to increment m and n.

It holds that

$$(\underline{\text{N}}\; i,\, j:\, m + 1 \leq i < I \;\wedge\; n \leq j < J:\, M(i,\, j) \geq 0)$$
$$= \quad \{\text{calculus}\}$$
$$(\underline{\text{N}}\; i,\, j:\, m \leq i < I \;\wedge\; n \leq j < J:\, M(i,\, j) \geq 0)$$
$$- \; (\underline{\text{N}}\; j:\, n \leq j < J:\, M(m,\, j) \geq 0)$$

Of this last expression, the first term is in **P**, so that we do not have to worry any more about that. For the second term, assuming that $M(m,\, n) \geq 0$, it holds that:

$$(\underline{\text{N}}\; j:\, n \leq j < J:\, M(m,\, j) \geq 0)$$
$$= \quad \{\text{because of the increase in value of } M \text{ in the second}$$
$$\text{argument, } M(m,\, n) \geq 0 \;\Rightarrow\; (\underline{\text{A}}\; j:\, n \leq j < N:$$
$$M(m,\, j) \geq 0) \text{ holds}\}$$
$$J - n$$

Thus we find that

$$\{P \;\wedge\; m \neq I \;\wedge\; n \neq J \;\wedge\; M(m,\, n) \geq 0\}$$
$$c := c + J - n;\; m := m + 1$$
$$\{P\}$$

For the case $M(m,\, n) < 0$ we try not to compute the term $(\underline{\text{N}}\; j:\, n \leq j < J:\, M(m,\, j) \geq 0)$ as yet, because this is far too complicated. First we look at a way to increment n.

In a completely analogous way, but this time using the decrease in value of **M** in the first argument, we find

$$\{P \;\wedge\; m \neq I \;\wedge\; n \neq J \;\wedge\; M(m,\, n) < 0\}$$
$$n := n + 1$$
$$\{P\}$$

so that for the inner block **S** we may choose

```
|[ m, n: int
; c, m, n:= 0, 0, 0
   {invariant P, variant function (I − m) + (J − n)}
; do m ≠ I ∧ n ≠ J
    → if M(m, n) ≥ 0 →  c:= c + J − n; m:= m + 1
      ▯  M(m, n) < 0 →  n:= n + 1
      fi
  od
]|
```

Index